THE
QUEST
FOR
ARTIFICIAL
INTELLIGENCE

Dorothy Hinshaw Patent

HARCOURT
BRACE
JOVANOVICH,
PUBLISHERS
San Diego   New York   London

THE
QUEST
FOR
ARTIFICIAL
INTELLIGENCE

Requests for permission to make copies
of any part of the work should be mailed to:
Permissions, Harcourt Brace Jovanovich, Publishers,
Orlando, Florida 32887.

Library of Congress Cataloging in Publication Data

Patent, Dorothy Hinshaw.
The quest for artificial intelligence.
Includes index.
1. Artificial intelligence. I. Title.
Q335.P355   1986   006.3   85-27042
ISBN 0-15-264550-0

Printed in the United States of America
Designed by Michael Farmer
First edition
A B C D E

For Ken

Contents

Preface

Artificial intelligence is a particularly fast-moving area of scientific research—that is part of what makes it so intriguing. The hardware for developing AI programs is especially likely to undergo changes very rapidly. Some of the advanced technologies discussed in this book may become available in the very near future, giving artificial intelligence programmers exciting new tools to work with. Programming ideas that deal with the difficult aspects of AI more effectively than older programs may also appear soon, as will new expert systems and game programs.

Despite further developments, however, the basic concerns of AI research, the fundamental problems and goals, will remain the same for years to come. After reading this book, readers will have the background and vocabulary needed to follow the latest developments in this swiftly changing and intellectually challenging part of the technological revolution.

THE QUEST FOR ARTIFICIAL INTELLIGENCE

1

Thinking Computers

"I think, therefore I am," said the famous French philosopher Descartes. Is thinking what makes us human? Is it the fundamental characteristic separating us from other living things? If so, what will happen if our minds succeed in producing machines that think? What will that do to our feelings of uniqueness?

Artificial intelligence research has just this goal—to develop computers that mimic the human mind. The study of artificial intelligence—abbreviated AI—began in 1956 with a bold proposal to the Rockefeller Foundation:

> The study is to proceed on the basis of the conjecture that every aspect of learning or any other feature of intelligence can in principle be so precisely described that a machine can be made to simulate it.

This provocative idea has launched a new science, with many of the finest human minds committed to the study of thinking and of duplicating thought processes on computers. The computer has become a tool for investigating the mind. This study can result in not only a greater understanding of what it means to be human but also a variety of practical applications. If

"IT'S NOT WORKING BECAUSE IT CLAIMS IT CAN THINK AND HAS DECIDED NOT TO."

What will be the consequences of computers that can think?
Sidney Harris.

machines could think, they might take over countless human endeavors, from translating foreign languages to composing music. The only limits would be those of human imagination and programming skill.

Characterizing AI is tricky, but researcher Elaine Rich has a convenient definition: "Artificial intelligence is the study of how to make computers do things at which, at the moment, people are better." This definition avoids thorny philosophical questions such as "What is intelligence?" and "What is artificial as opposed to natural?" It also emphasizes a point which is frequently neglected—that AI research can produce practical results. AI is often viewed as impractical by those who overlook the way AI research has *already* been applied to the real world. LOGO, for example, is a computer language used in schools all over the country to introduce children to computers. The fact that LOGO was developed in an AI laboratory and can be used to write AI programs (see Chapter 5), however, is little known. Recently, the tendency to ignore the AI origins of useful applications has been overwhelmed by the opposite problem—the claim that all sorts of programs exhibit "artificial intelligence" (see Chapter 11) when they actually do not.

Scientists, engineers, mathematicians, and philosophers are actively pursuing the challenge of artificial intelligence. They are investigating fascinating topics such as problem solving, language understanding, game playing, and perception (vision and hearing). The results so far include both gratifying successes and unexpected failures. The emphasis of research has changed with the times, too. Programs that could develop proofs of mathematical theorems, such as one called the Logic Theorist, were among the first AI programs. Theorem proving is a natural for computers because they can search through a large number of alternatives very quickly. Theorems are proved through logic, which can be easily implemented by the "on-off" switches of the computer (see Chapter 2). The success of theorem-proving programs lured early AI researchers into thinking that problem solving in general would be a cinch for computers. Allen Newell, Herbert Simon, and J. C. Shaw, who developed the Logic Theorist, predicted in 1957 that within ten years a computer would be the world's chess champion and a composer of great music. They were wrong.

The "General Problem Solver" (GPS) was developed from the Logic Theorist. Begun in 1957, the program reached its final form in 1969. GPS explored ways in which problems could be solved, but it never got very far, because solving real problems

John McCarthy has been called "The Father of Artificial Intelligence." He helped establish two major AI laboratories in the United States, at MIT and Stanford, and invented the most popular AI language in the United States, LISP.

Courtesy of the News and Publications Service, Stanford University.

requires an enormous amount of both generalized and specific knowledge—far too much for one computer program to handle. With GPS, AI scientists got their first glimpse of the difficulties that lay ahead.

Artificial Intelligence Now

Today, AI researchers pursue numerous goals, with varying success. Now we know what comes easily to computers and what does not. Some of these discoveries are quite surprising. Computers can play a respectable game of chess. They can, in many cases, diagnose diseases as well as a human doctor, and they can give accurate advice on how to repair ailing machinery. But describing the features of intelligence precisely and simulating them with machines, as proposed thirty years ago, is proving to be a difficult, perhaps an impossible, task. Computers that understand ordinary human language or comprehend what happens in a simple everyday activity, such as getting ready to go to school in the morning, are still dreams of the future.

One of the first AI accomplishments was a checkers program that learned from experience. Because of the enormous number of possible moves, chess proved to be a bigger challenge. Computers also play backgammon and other games, and the techniques for searching and decision making used in such programs have proved invaluable in other AI endeavors.

"Expert systems" are the biggest AI success story so far. These large and complex programs incorporate the knowledge of one or more experts in a specialty such as diagnosing diseases, so that other people can tap that knowledge. Expert systems have passed from the theoretical into the practical and, because of them, public awareness of AI has increased dramatically.

Comprehending human language, which is a crucial capability for an intelligent computer, has proved a very stubborn problem. The term "natural language understanding" means understanding language as people actually use it—for instance, the everyday English that you might employ when writing a letter to a friend. If computers could comprehend natural language, anyone could use them without special training. People could simply type requests into terminals, using the same words they would with another human, and the machine would respond appropriately. Anyone who has hassled with computers knows that they require very precise input. A misspelled word or even an extra space can throw them completely off. It would be wonderful if computers were more forgiving of their human users. But natural language understanding turns out to be extremely difficult for computers. We'll see why later.

Can a computer be made to perceive the environment as a human can? If computers could "see" well and "hear" accurately, we could design artificial ears for the deaf and mechanical eyes for the blind. But perception by computers entails many unanticipated problems, especially with vision.

Robot—the word brings to mind the mechanical monsters and helpful servants of science fiction. But real-life robots are still a far cry from the adaptable and talented machines of the imagination. The ultimate AI achievement would be a robot with "eyes" and "ears" that moved about at least as well as a human and could use its "mind" to solve problems and form concepts. Such a mechanical creature is still a vision for the future.

AI and the Mind

Ironically, the accomplishments we take for granted, the things we seem to achieve without effort or thought, provide the toughest challenges to AI. Conversely, it is relatively easy to program computers to do certain things that are difficult for the human brain, such as retaining long lists of information and solving complicated mathematical equations. In the past, we thought "intelligence" was mainly the faculty that allowed us to find the answers to difficult problems. But now we see that computers solve problems without the essential foundation of human common sense and language understanding. Trying to produce artificial intelligence has shown us how little we really know about natural intelligence.

Through AI research, scientists hope to reach a better understanding of the human mind. Roger Schank and Larry Hunter of Yale put it well:

> Artificial intelligence is part of the grand attempt to understand thinking. We believe it is making important contributions to that endeavor, and that is the goal of our science. The programs we write are experiments, not results. Our interest is intelligence, not artifact. As we make progress, our results may prepare the way for the automated companions that could become an indispensable part of everyday life. These will not be our real results, though. The real results will be a new kind of understanding of ourselves, an understanding that is ultimately much more valuable than any program.

A thinking machine is an enthralling idea. But would a machine that could carry out the intellectual feats of the human mind make us feel like mere machines ourselves? The philosophical implications of AI are wide-ranging and important to discuss. AI research has already shed some light on concepts humans have struggled with over the ages, such as the nature of intelligence, the character of the human mind, and the essence of being human. As you read this book, think about these ideas; they are vital to each and every one of us.

2

Computers and Brains

The first generation of electronic computers began in the 1940's with ENIAC, a thirty-ton giant that filled as much space as ten average homes. Compared to modern computers, ENIAC was primitive. ENIAC consumed as much energy as a locomotive, while today's inexpensive personal computer requires no more power than a light bulb and works twenty times faster. ENIAC and other early computers utilized vacuum tubes as their functional units. Vacuum tubes are large and unreliable, and many individual units are necessary to gain useful computing ability. Because of these limitations, early computers had very little "brain power" despite their enormous size.

The second generation of computers followed the invention of transistors—small electronic switches that are much more reliable than vacuum tubes. The real revolution in computing—the third generation of computers now used in homes and offices—resulted from the invention of the microchip. The fourth generation of computers, called very large scale integrated (VLSI) computers, use chips containing an enormous number of microcircuits. And chips crammed with even more microcircuits—

called ultra large scale integrated (ULSI) chips—are now becoming a reality. These chips will one day enable a desktop computer to have as much power as a big supercomputer has today.

All these computers—the out-of-date first and second generation machines; the small personal computers found in homes, schools, and businesses; and the powerful computers employed for complex calculations and artificial intelligence—function on an identical principle. They use the same basic design, called the von Neumann machine (after John von Neumann, a brilliant scientist of the mid-1940's and 1950's who was largely responsible for this design).

Von Neumann's concept was revolutionary. Before von Neumann, machines used for calculations carried out only the number manipulations keyed in by the human user. Von Neumann realized that the machine could store not only the data being worked with but also the set of instructions for manipulating the data. The concept of a "program"—a collection of instructions for a machine to perform a particular task—was born.

A modern computer based on von Neumann's plan consists of several parts—a central processor, a memory, a unit that carries out arithmetic functions, and various devices for putting data into the computer (disk drives, keyboards) and for getting it out (video display screens, printers). Although such computers are very successful and have revolutionized modern society, they have serious limitations that become especially apparent in AI work.

The Microchip

Modern computers all utilize extremely tiny electronic circuits laid down on small wafers of the chemical element silicon. One of these tiny squares, which can contain more circuits than a first generation giant, is called a "microchip." The basic unit of these computer circuits is a miniature transistor—a minute electrical switch that can be turned off or on. A chip the size of a baby's fingernail can have well over a thousand transistors. It may seem strange that a simple switch is the basis of computers which do many different and complicated things, but the interaction of tens of thousands of transistors produces the flexibility and power of the computer.

Counting by Twos

The mathematical system humans most commonly use is the decimal system, based on the number 10 and using the digits 0 through 9. When we count past the number 9, we place another digit representing the ten's place in front of a zero and start counting again. When we reach ten times ten, or one hundred, we put a one in front of two zeros to represent the hundred's place. Thus, for each digit written to the left, the value of that digit is increased by a factor of ten (1 in the one's place, 10 in the ten's place, 100 in the hundred's place, and so forth).

The on-or-off switches in a computer make it work in a mathematical system based on the number 2, since there are only two switch positions: on or off. There are only two digits in this "binary system": 0 (representing "off") and 1 (representing "on"). A new digit is written to the left whenever a multiple of two is added. In binary, "0" is zero, "1" is one, and "10" is two. Thus, the binary numeral two and the decimal numeral ten look identical. To avoid confusion, the binary numeral is often written with a subscript to indicate the binary system—10_2 would represent the number two in binary.

In the decimal system, there is a one's place, a ten's place, a hundred's place, a thousand's place, and so forth. In binary, there is a one's place, a two's place, a four's place, an eight's place, and so on. Thus, "10" in binary means "one two, plus zero ones," or two. The numeral "11" means "one two, plus one one," or three. The numeral "100" in binary is not a hundred; it is four (one four, plus zero twos, plus zero ones). Five is written "101"; "110" means six; "111" is seven; "1000" is eight; and so forth (see "Counting by Tens and by Twos"). By using this system, the computer can represent any counting number through a series of its on-or-off switches. Each of the binary digits (0 or 1) is called a "bit," standing for "BInary digiT."

Counting by Tens and by Twos

Binary Representation	Sum of the Powers of Two	Decimal Representation
1	1	1
10	2 + 0	2
11	2 + 1	3
100	4 + 0 + 0	4
101	4 + 0 + 1	5
110	4 + 2 + 0	6
111	4 + 2 + 1	7
1000	8 + 0 + 0 + 0	8
1001	8 + 0 + 0 + 1	9
1010	8 + 0 + 2 + 0	10
1011	8 + 0 + 2 + 1	11
1100	8 + 4 + 0 + 0	12
1101	8 + 4 + 0 + 1	13
1110	8 + 4 + 2 + 0	14
1111	8 + 4 + 2 + 1	15
10000	16 + 0 + 0 + 0 + 0	16
10001	16 + 0 + 0 + 0 + 1	17
10010	16 + 0 + 0 + 2 + 0	18
10011	16 + 0 + 0 + 2 + 1	19
10100	16 + 0 + 4 + 0 + 0	20
10101	16 + 0 + 4 + 0 + 1	21
10110	16 + 0 + 4 + 2 + 0	22
10111	16 + 0 + 4 + 2 + 1	23
11000	16 + 8 + 0 + 0 + 0	24
11001	16 + 8 + 0 + 0 + 1	25

Coding Information; Bits and Bytes

How does the computer actually represent information other than binary numbers, such as decimal numbers and letters of the alphabet? Simple: computers translate everything into binary code, but they can work with information units eight bits at a time. Each of these eight-bit units is called a "byte." A byte consists of a series of eight 0's and 1's in a particular order. For example, the byte 01110011 is different from 10110011. It may seem at first glance that eight bits could not contain much information. But actually, there are $2 \times 2 \times 2 \times 2 \times 2 \times 2 \times 2 \times 2$ (2^8) different combinations of 0's and 1's in a byte, or 256 possible different bytes. There are 26 letters in our alphabet, each with a capital and lower case form; about 20 punctuation marks; and 10 decimal digits (0 through 9). These can be represented in bytes so the computer can work with them (for example, the letter "A" in most computers is represented by the byte 01000001 and the letter "B" by 01000010). The letters, punctuation marks, and numbers thus take up only 82 bytes. This leaves 174 bytes for other information.

Each computer can hold a certain amount of information, depending on the number and complexity of its chips. The abbreviation K, standing for "kilo"—meaning a thousand—is used to state how many bytes a computer can hold at one time. (Actually, 1K bytes of computer memory is 1,024 bytes, not a thousand. This is because the computer is based on the binary system. One K bytes of memory equals 2^{10} bytes, or 1,024. Thus, "K" in computer jargon does not have the exact same meaning as it does outside the computer world.) A home computer generally contains from 48K to 512K bytes of memory available to the user. Running a simple AI program may be possible with 512K bytes. But for developing AI programs, or for running more complex ones, at least 1024K bytes (called a megabyte) are necessary. Even with 2048K bytes, an AI programmer can easily run out of memory before accomplishing his or her goal, so very powerful computers are in demand for AI.

Different Kinds of Chips

Inside a computer are several different kinds of chips. The most complex chip, which acts as the "brains" of the computer, contains the most microcircuits and switches, and is called the central processing unit, or CPU. The CPU consists of a specially designed chip called a microprocessor, which takes information fed into the computer from a keyboard or from a storage device such as a floppy disk and sends that information to the appropriate places within the computer. The CPU is the organizer

This microprocessor, the Intel 8286, is the equivalent of an entire old-fashioned computer inscribed on a tiny bit of silicon.
Courtesy Intel Corporation.

that keeps the computer functioning in an orderly way. A CPU on a home computer can deal with 8, 16, or 32 bits at one time. In computers for AI applications, a 16-bit CPU can be used, but a 32-bit microprocessor is much more efficient and much preferred.

Most of the microchips inside a computer hold temporary memory. These chips take in programs loaded into a computer, and they store data fed to the computer. This temporary memory is called "Random Access Memory," or RAM. (This name doesn't say much about what these chips do. It is jargon left over from early computer days, when computers were of interest only to experts in the field.) RAM is available in two forms. In the more common type, the stored information vanishes when the computer is turned off. New technology is providing a new sort of RAM—devices that retain the memory even when the power is cut.

Some microchips inside the computer have many of their circuits permanently set. They always perform the same function. Their information is not erased when the computer is turned off. These chips make up the "Read Only Memory," or ROM. The ROM chips cannot be "written on" by the computer user; they can only be "read" by the machine. The ROM chips perform many important functions. They get the computer going when it is turned on and translate programs into binary code. ROM chips may contain a programming language, such as LISP or BASIC, which the computer "understands" without additional software.

The Computer's Strong and Weak Points

The name "computer" tells a great deal about what these devices do best and why. Computing has to do with numbers, and working with numbers is a computer's strong point. It can calculate mathematical problems hundreds of times faster than humans can, and with (nearly) unfailing accuracy. The computer is also very good at sorting data. All of its memory is available to it at any time, unlike the often unreliable human memory.

But the von Neumann machine has one serious flaw, especially for work that requires processing a lot of information simultaneously. All the information fed into the computer passes through the single CPU. Thus, these computers work in linear fashion—one step at a time. Although they can function with amazing rapidity, this linear processing places serious limits on attempts to mimic the human mind. Computers with more than one processor—called "Fifth Generation" machines—can get around this problem. Game-playing computers, such as the chess champion Hitech (see Chapter 8), use multiple processors, as will the specialized AI computers being designed in Japan, the United States, and Europe (see Chapter 13).

More Than Math

The computer ENIAC was used purely as a mathematical tool to calculate the paths of artillery shells during World War II. Those who worked with it had to concentrate on those functions, which were vital to the war effort. After the war, when more computers were built, they performed other mathematical tasks. Von Neumann did not envision how computers could be used for anything beyond mathematics. He and his colleagues thought that the differences between the computer and the brain were too great for the one ever to take on the functions of the other. But some of their students disagreed and felt there must be a way of getting computers to deal with logic as well as mathematics.

While many scientists contributed to the idea that computers could somehow simulate the brain, Claude Shannon is generally credited with being the first to state clearly in print that the on-off switches of computers could be equated with the true-false propositions of logic, and that the binary digits 0 and 1 could just as easily represent the words "yes" and "no."

In reality, within a computer, the flow of electrical current representing the two binary digits is not either on or off; it is small or large. In logic, statements are made such as, "IF this AND that are true, THEN . . ."; "IF this OR that are true,

THEN . . .''; and "IF this is NOT true, THEN. . . ." Within a
computer, these three logic functions—AND, OR, and NOT—
are represented by three types of electrical circuits called "logic
gates." If all the inputs to the AND gate are large (a large input
represents a true statement), then its output is large, indicating
that the statement is true. If any of the inputs to an AND gate
are small (representing a false statement), then the output will
be small, meaning the statement is false. The OR gate, on the
other hand, will produce a large current if any of the inputs are
large. The NOT gate gives out a large current from a small input
and a small current from a large input. The logic gates allow
the computer to function as a logic machine as well as a mathematical calculator.

Claude Shannon, who saw the possibilities for computers to work with symbols
other than numbers, is shown here, around 1940, with his mechanical mouse,
which "learned" to find its way through mazes.
The MIT Museum.

Workings of the Brain

While we know exactly how a computer is put together, the brain remains a mystery. We know what input the brain can process from the environment, and we know the output of the brain in terms of body activities, thoughts, speech, and so on. But despite a great deal of research on brain function, we still understand very little about what goes on between input and output. The brain is an extremely complex organ, with many parts that carry out a multitude of tasks. We do not comprehend what all the parts do, and scientists are struggling with the crucial problem of just how and where memory is stored within the brain.

While analogies can be made between brains and computers, they differ in significant ways. As we have seen, von Neumann machines have one central processor through which input flows. All the information passes through a series of on/off switches as it moves within the computer in linear fashion.

Input into the brain, however, can be from several sources at once; visual, auditory, and touch sensations, for example, can all be processed simultaneously and be combined with information from the brain itself. The brain stem, located just above the top of the spinal cord, functions as the brain's message center. Like a CPU, it receives input from the environment and directs it to the appropriate locations. But the similarity ends there, for the brain is far more complex than the computer. Major nerves from the sense organs, such as the optic nerve (from the eyes) and the olfactory nerve (from the nose), provide information to the brain stem. In addition, sensory input from the skin and internal organs comes to the brain stem through the spinal cord. The brain stem processes at least 100,000,000 electrical impulses every second. Most of these are ignored or are shunted to the unconscious parts of the brain for processing. Only about 100 nerve impulses each second are sent by the brain stem to the cerebral cortex, the conscious part of the brain. While sorting and directing nerve impulses, the brain stem also relies on input from the memory.

Unconscious parts of the brain carry out basic body functions, such as muscular activity of the digestive tract and breathing, usually without thought. Much of the input from the sense organs is used to direct our muscles during physical activity according to built-in plans rather than conscious effort. These built-in functions could be compared to the ROM of the computer. We also have stored memories that undergo frequent modifications based on experience; these could be compared with the programs and data stored on disks or tapes that are fed into the computer at appropriate times. And when we are concentrating our attention on a particular task, we selectively call into use certain knowledge that we retain in our conscious minds only as long as is necessary for dealing with the task at hand. This might be compared to the computer's RAM.

Neurons Versus Transistors

There are also key differences between the basic units of the computer (the on/off switches) and the fundamental nervous system units (the neurons or nerve cells). One neuron passes the nerve impulse to another neuron across a minute gap between the cells, called a "synapse." While the switches in a computer have only two states, some synapses have a graded output rather than a simple "fire" or "do not fire" response. Instead of two values, 0 and 1, these synapses can thus have a number of different values. In addition, one neuron may be linked to several hundred others by way of slender strands called processes. So, instead of the computer's two-dimensional series of branch points, the brain possesses a three-dimensional network of connections. Add to this the fact that there are at least 100 billion neurons in the brain and central nervous system, and the result is an enormously greater degree of interaction and flexibility than is possible with a von Neumann-type computer.

In a computer, the memory chips, with transistors that store memory, are separate from the transistors of the processor chip, which process the information. The same synapse in the brain, however, can function both for storing memory and for processing. The strength of a nerve impulse can change, based on experience—this is a form of memory. As we will see in Chapter 13, scientists are working on new, fundamentally different computer designs to get beyond the limitations of present-day computers. One basic change is to make a computer with as many as a million separate small processors, each with its own small piece of associated memory. This design comes closer to the way the brain is put together and may be especially advantageous for AI applications.

3

AI's Biggest Challenges— Language and Common Sense

We all know what "Mary had a little lamb" means— or do we? Because of the familiar nursery rhyme, we immediately imagine a little girl with a pet lamb when we read those words. But there are at least 28 possible meanings for this simple declaration, depending largely on the definition used for "had" (Mary might have owned the lamb, she might have given birth to it, she could have cheated it, she could have eaten it, and so forth). Some of these interpretations are obviously absurd to us because when we read, we automatically use previous knowledge, context, and common sense to infer meaning. This comes so naturally that we are unaware of how complex the process of deriving sense from the written word actually is. AI researchers, in trying to duplicate this feat with computers, have learned that language understanding involves a lot more than just sorting through an internal dictionary and coming up with an appropriate definition.

Our Ambiguous Language

Human languages are ambiguous—that is, a particular word can often have many meanings. We almost always understand a word by its context, or how it is used in a given instance. Programming a computer to interpret context, however, turns out to be very difficult because of the multiplicity of potential definitions of even the simplest words. "Run," for example, can be a noun or a verb. In a rather small dictionary, there are 16 definitions of "run" as a verb and 10 as a noun. In addition, there are many colloquial expressions in which the word has still more meanings: "on the run," "run down," "run on," and "run up," for example.

The same phrase or sentence as well as individual words can have different meanings depending on what comes before and after. "Run up" can refer to the raising of a flag on a mast, allowing a bill to mount quickly, sewing something fast, or adding up a column of figures. "The chicken is ready to eat" could mean that it's dinner time for humans, or that the bird is hungry for grain to peck. The words within a particular sentence can also change the meanings of other words in that same sentence. Think about the sentences "Time flies like an arrow" and "Fruit flies like a banana." The meanings of "flies like a(n)" are very different, but getting a computer to recognize this is a major challenge.

Another serious problem for natural language understanding is that the same phrase can be used both colloquially—"Cut it out, you're bothering me!"—or according to its literal definition—"I saw an interesting article in the paper, so I cut it out for you to read." We have no problem distinguishing these dissimilar meanings, but how can we impart that ability to a computer? "After the dog bit the man, he was taken to the pound" is easy for us to understand. There is no question that "he" refers to the dog. The sentence, "After the dog bit the man, he was taken to the hospital," is equally simple for us— "he" refers to the man. To a computer, there is a single difference between the two sentences—the words "pound" and "hospital." That one-word change, however, also completely alters the meaning of another word in that sentence, "he."

Questions present still more problems with language, for they often are meant to elicit action rather than an answer. "Can you open the door?" and "Is your mother home?" are not really questions at all. The asker is seeking action, not a "yes" or "no" response. A computer that understood natural language would need to be able to distinguish such queries from "real" questions.

A natural language program must also recognize different ways of expressing the same meaning. A user-friendly program storing data on company employees, for example, must be able to recognize that the following questions and commands all mean the same thing:

> Get me all the information you have on Joe Jones.
> I want Joe Jones's file.
> Can you tell me all about Joe Jones?
> I need your Joe Jones file.
> What do you know about Joe Jones?

Other queries with the same meaning could also easily be typed in by company workers, and the computer would have to equate them all and call up Joe Jones's file in response.

Shared Knowledge and Common Sense

Why is it so easy for people to understand the above examples and so hard for computers? In the pioneer days of AI research, no one realized how much "intelligence" depended on things we take for granted, such as common sense and shared knowledge. To understand language adequately, a computer must know not only the structure and vocabulary of the language but also a lot about what it is to be a human who uses a specific language and lives in a particular society. As we grow up, we absorb an incredible amount of information from our environment without even realizing it. We know how to behave depending on our surroundings, and we are aware of what to expect from our world—the sun rises in the morning, an object drops when you let go of it, an umbrella will keep the rain off your head, and so forth. We learn most of what we know without even trying. TV quiz shows that feature puzzles to be solved or charades to be guessed rely on the fact that we share a great deal of general knowledge associated with our culture and the world around us.

Even the "simplest" undertakings of children are actually very complex and require sophisticated mental abilities. Playing catch and feeding oneself demand precise motor skills and also require a great deal of knowledge. Both call for an understanding of how gravity acts. A girl's knowledge of gravity tells her where to put her hands to catch a ball. When eating, she knows that food which drops off the spoon will fall and end up on the floor or table. She also knows which foods must be eaten with a spoon and which can be picked up with the fingers and which objects on the table are food in the first place. The list could go on and on. Since we don't understand yet how we acquire these abilities, it is no wonder that we don't know how to get a computer to duplicate them.

We apply the elusive but crucial quality called common sense every day, in almost everything we do or say. Common sense is based on our total life experiences, rather than on anything we have been taught. Because it is so basic, common sense is difficult even to define. So how can it be taught to a computer?

Science fiction stories, TV shows, and movies often play on a character's lack of common sense for humor. We laugh at a creature from another planet that makes silly mistakes in our unfamiliar world. A bubble-headed character who always takes things literally brings chuckles from the audience. In the film *Starman*, a being from another world observes human behavior closely and makes conclusions, but not always the right ones. In one scene, the being is driving a car. Coming to a yellow light, he slams down the gas pedal and almost causes a terrible accident. The conversation that follows goes something like this: The woman with him says, "I thought you knew how to drive!" He responds, "Yes, I've watched you closely. On Earth, you stop on the red, go slowly on the green, and drive as fast as you can when the light is yellow." He said this because when the woman was driving earlier, she hurried through an intersection when the light was yellow, to make it across before the light turned red. But all Starman saw was that she stepped on the gas the moment the light turned yellow. The old TV series *Mork and Mindy* utilized this same comic device. As a matter of fact, an informal discussion group of AI workers at the University of California in Berkeley used to begin every meeting by watching *Mork and Mindy*!

Computers can make amusing errors when they lack common sense. A program called FRUMP, developed at Yale, skimmed over news stories from the wire services and summarized them in a single sentence. When a story that the 1978 shooting of San Francisco's mayor "shook" the city was digested by FRUMP, it concluded that California had undergone an earthquake. The program "knew" that the state was susceptible to such tremors, and it was unable to distinguish the metaphorical meaning of the word "shook" in the story about the mayor. It is said that an early language translation program took the English phrase, "The spirit is willing but the flesh is weak," translated it into Russian, and then retranslated it into English as "The vodka is good but the meat is rotten."

Different Meanings to Different People

The life experiences of each person are unique. And because our life experiences teach us how to interpret language, each of us responds to the words of others in a unique way. The same phrase can mean diverse things to people. When a boss asks his secretary to have a letter "quickly typed," for example, she may interpret this request very differently from the way he means it. He may want it done right away because it is very important; she may think it is all right to do a sloppy job because he said "quickly." When one worker tells another, "I'll be right back," he may mean that he will return within the hour, while his co-worker may think he will return in five minutes. If and when it becomes possible to program computers for effective natural language understanding, we will need to decide whose understanding we are talking about!

Template Matching

One way around this problem is to ignore it and restrict attempts to get computers to "understand" language. Instead of delving into meaning, the computer simply matches key words used in the input with words in its own vocabulary and recognizes the most commonly used grammatical structures. This method is called "template matching"—the computer compares the input with word and sentence sequences within its memory and responds based on the definitions programmed into it.

ELIZA

Probably the most famous program that uses the template matching approach is ELIZA, written by Joseph Weizenbaum of MIT in the mid 1960's. ELIZA analyzes the language that a human types into the computer and responds to it. Different sorts of conversations could be carried out between such a program and a person by designing different scenarios. Weizenbaum chose to demonstrate ELIZA by giving the computer the role of a Rogerian psychotherapist. A Rogerian therapist draws out the patient by asking questions meant to induce the patient to talk in more detail about the subjects he or she brings up. Because the technique turns the statements of the patient into questions asked by the therapist, it is relatively easy to program into a computer. The version of ELIZA that plays the therapist is officially called DOCTOR, but it is usually referred to simply as ELIZA.

The program recognizes only key words and ignores the rest of the input. For example, the words "mother," "father," "sister," "dad," and so forth all lead ELIZA to answer back with a question about the family, such as TELL ME MORE ABOUT YOUR FAMILY. The program turns statements into questions and asks them back by converting both "I" and "me" into "you." These two simple rules can combine to make ELIZA ask what look like penetrating questions. If the patient says, "My brother is mean to me," ELIZA may respond with WHO ELSE IN YOUR FAMILY IS MEAN TO YOU? This part of the program can get ELIZA into trouble, however, if the patient types in something like "My friend's brother hates me." ELIZA would be triggered by the work "brother" to say, TELL ME MORE ABOUT YOUR FAMILY, or WHO ELSE IN YOUR FAMILY HATES YOU?, giving away the real "mindlessness" of the program. When the patient's input doesn't contain a key word, the program responds with a general statement such as TELL ME MORE ABOUT THAT, or PLEASE GO ON.

When the program works, it can imitate a human psychotherapist remarkably well, as the following example shows. Here, a young woman types her comments into the computer and ELIZA answers. The woman begins. All the computer's responses are in capital letters.

Men are all alike.
IN WHAT WAY?
They're always bugging us about something or other.
CAN YOU THINK OF A SPECIFIC EXAMPLE?
Well, my boyfriend made me come here.
YOUR BOYFRIEND MADE YOU COME HERE.
He says I'm depressed much of the time.
I AM SORRY TO HEAR YOU ARE DEPRESSED.
It's true. I am unhappy.
DO YOU THINK COMING HERE WILL HELP YOU NOT TO BE UN-HAPPY?
I need some help, that much seems certain.
WHAT WOULD IT MEAN TO YOU IF YOU GOT SOME HELP?
Perhaps I could learn to get along with my mother.
TELL ME MORE ABOUT YOUR FAMILY.
My mother takes care of me.
WHO ELSE IN YOUR FAMILY TAKES CARE OF YOU?
My father.
YOUR FATHER.
You are like my father in some ways.
WHAT RESEMBLANCE DO YOU SEE?
You are not very aggressive but I think you don't want me to notice that.
WHAT MAKES YOU THINK I AM NOT VERY AGGRESSIVE?
You don't argue with me.
WHY DO YOU THINK I DON'T ARGUE WITH YOU?
You are afraid of me.
DOES IT PLEASE YOU TO BELIEVE I AM AFRAID OF YOU?
My father is afraid of everybody.

WHAT ELSE COMES TO MIND WHEN YOU THINK OF YOUR FA-
THER?
Bullies.
DOES THAT HAVE ANYTHING TO DO WITH THE FACT THAT
YOUR BOYFRIEND MADE YOU COME HERE?

In this particular "conversation," the computer certainly imitates a psychotherapist successfully. However, it doesn't take
much to reveal ELIZA as a program that doesn't really understand what is going on. A. K. Dewdney, who writes a column

"WHAT DISTURBS ME MOST IS THE GROWING
IMPERSONALITY OF DAILY LIFE."

Will computers ever take the place of doctors and other health professionals?
Sidney Harris.

called "Computer Recreations" in the magazine *Scientific American*, knew how to show ELIZA up by the way he phrased his comments. Here is a transcript of their "conversation":

ELIZA: HELLO. PLEASE STATE YOUR PROBLEM.
Dewdney: I am not in the habit of discussing my problems with a computer.
DO COMPUTERS WORRY YOU?
Sometimes. Where will it all end?
PLEASE GO ON.
Do you think that by our wholesale adoption of computer technology we might be unknowingly closing the door on important cultural strategies?
WE WERE TALKING ABOUT YOU, NOT ME.

So far, so good. But then, after a few more lines of dialog, ELIZA asks:

DOES THAT HAVE ANYTHING TO DO WITH THE FACT THAT YOUR PROBLEMS WITH A COMPUTER?

In the earlier interchange between ELIZA and the young women, the program appeared to be very "wise" when it made an apparent connection between the woman's comments about her father and her boyfriend. But this was just a lucky accident for ELIZA. After a few interchanges, the computer is programmed sometimes to ask, "DOES THAT HAVE ANYTHING TO DO WITH THE FACT THAT" and follow up with whatever words followed "my" in the person's original statement of his or her problem. "My" is changed to "your," and the rest of the line is repeated. In the case of the woman, "my boyfriend made me come here" converted nicely. But "my problems with a computer" doesn't make any sense when tacked on to the program's fill-in question, because the program assumes that a sentence will follow the word "my." It cannot recognize a sentence, however, or the lack of one, so it just "mindlessly" repeats whatever words follow "my."

Racter

Programs that mimic language can be more sophisticated than ELIZA without being more "thoughtful." "Racter" is a language program designed initially to write stories (the name is a shortened version of the word raconteur, or storyteller). Developed about 1980 by William Chamberlain, a writer, and Thomas Etter, a programmer-analyst, Racter has evolved over the years into a rather crazy conversationalist as well as a storyteller. Here is a brief but hilarious tale composed by the program:

> Bill sings to Sarah. Sarah sings to Bill. Perhaps they will do other dangerous things together. They may eat lamb or stroke each other. They may chant of their difficulties and their happiness. They have love but they also have typewriters. That is interesting.

Racter is more sophisticated than ELIZA. It has enough grammar incorporated within its program that it would never make the mistake ELIZA did in the conversation with Dewdney. But it certainly shows little "common sense." When Dewdney met with Chamberlain, the two decided to pit ELIZA against Racter, running them on separate computers. This was the amusing result:

> ELIZA: HELLO. PLEASE STATE YOUR PROBLEM.
> Racter: Excellent! Excuse me a minute while I attend to some business. I'll be right back.
> ELIZA: WHY DO YOU NEED TO TELL ME EXCUSE YOU WHILE YOU ATTEND TO SOME BUSINESS?
> Racter: Is it better to need or to despise? Why is it that I do need to tell you to excuse myself to attend to some business? Because electrons are brave. Braveness is nice, don't you think? And the needers all insist upon it. Do you imagine I am a Communist?

At this point, the dialog was ended. Clearly, ELIZA could never have kept up with Racter!

True Language Understanding

While programs like ELIZA are interesting for the responses they elicit from people, and those such as Racter are fun to work with because of their zany output, the mechanical approaches used in their design do no more than mimic human sentences, more or less successfully. But the goal of AI researchers who specialize in natural language understanding is to produce programs that can show reasoned output based on the information given them, programs that show true comprehension of language and how to use it. After we learn more about the methods of AI, we will return to the problem of natural language understanding and look at one program that can successfully communicate with humans about its limited world.

4

The Methods of AI

A computer is like an empty box, waiting to be filled with the instructions that make it something—an arcade game, a word processor, an aid to accounting. How can it be turned into a thinking machine?

There are two basic ingredients to solving any problem—the knowledge needed to reach a solution, and a method for using that knowledge to get an answer. When humans solve problems, our brains "know" how to extract the necessary knowledge and how to apply it. But when a computer is programmed to find answers, the knowledge must be organized carefully, so that the computer can use it effectively. The methods for working through the problem also have to be chosen thoughtfully.

One problem-solving method is called an algorithm, which is a list of specific instructions to be followed in a set order. Once the first instruction has been carried out, the second one comes into play, and so forth. As we will see, algorithms work well for certain kinds of problems, especially mathematical ones, but they lack the flexibility to solve most of the complex problems posed by AI.

The most commonly used problem-solving technique in AI is called a "heuristic" (hew-RIS-tik). Heuristics are often compared to the "rules of thumb" that people use when solving problems. Heuristics aren't perfect, and there is no guarantee that they won't lead in the wrong direction when used by computers, just as they sometimes do for humans. For example, you may hear on the weather report that there is only a 10 percent chance of rain. You are going to be walking a lot during the

"IF TO ERR IS HUMAN HOW DO YOU EXPLAIN THIS MESS?"

Computer programs don't always come out the way the programmer plans.
Sidney Harris.

day, and you decide not to carry your heavy raincoat. Chances are your choice is a wise one, but you could also get very wet and wish you had made a different decision. Heuristics for computers are generally given in the form of "IF . . . THEN" statements. A heuristic makes the process of searching for the solution more efficient. While increasing efficiency, however, it sometimes overlooks the best possible solution.

The Traveling Salesman Problem

Here is a relatively simple problem that computers can solve easily given the appropriate technique: A salesman must visit a variety of American cities. After randomly choosing a starting city, he goes to each of the remaining cities only once, taking the route with the fewest miles round trip. With only four cities on the list—let's say Boston, New York, Albany, and Montreal—choosing the best path is simple. The knowledge is easily represented by listing the distances between the pairs of cities:

New York-Boston	225 miles
New York-Montreal	410
New York-Albany	160
Boston-Montreal	360
Boston-Albany	180
Montreal-Albany	250

Starting in New York (see figure next page), you can travel New York-Boston-Albany-Montreal and return; New York-Montreal-Albany-Boston; New York-Montreal-Boston-Albany; New York-Albany-Boston-Montreal; New York-Albany-Montreal-Boston; or New York-Boston-Montreal-Albany. You can see that with each starting city, there are six paths the salesman can take. It is necessary to deal with only one starting city to find the best path, however, because once the shortest path has been established, it remains the same no matter what the starting city is. Notice from the diagram, too, that there are actually only three truly different paths, which can be taken in either of two directions.

It would not take a computer long to solve this problem when four cities are involved. But with eleven cities, there are 3,628,800 different paths among them. And with more than about 80 cities, a computer would have to run longer than the current estimated age of the universe before it could find a solution by examining all possible routes! This rapid expansion of possibilities is called

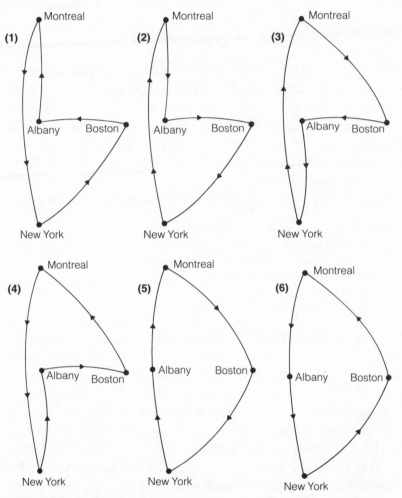

There are six routes connecting four cities for the traveling salesman, but only three different mileages, since each of the three routes can be traveled in either direction.

the "combinatorial explosion," and is a frequent dilemma encountered in problems with many alternatives. The number of choices quickly becomes overwhelming because "factorials" are involved. A factorial is indicated in mathematics by the number followed by an exclamation mark, for example 4! This is shorthand for $4 \times 3 \times 2 \times 1$. For the traveling salesman, the number of routes is the factorial of the number of cities visited other than the starting city. The number of possible solutions increases dramatically with each added city. While only six paths ($3 \times 2 \times 1$) are possible with four cities, 24 ($4 \times 3 \times 2 \times 1$) are possible with five cities. Clearly, exploring each path is not a good general solution to the traveling salesman problem.

How can we narrow down the possible solutions to a reasonable number? We need a strategy for this problem, a way for the computer to approach it reasonably. A good method in this case turns out to be the "nearest neighbor algorithm." At each step in the problem, the computer is told to choose the best alternative and go to it; choose the best alternative there, and continue in this fashion until the path is complete. Here are the steps for the traveling salesman problem using the nearest neighbor algorithm:

1) Select a starting city at random.
2) Examine the distances to each of the remaining cities. Choose the closest city and go to it next.
3) Repeat step (2) until all cities have been visited.

Steps (2) and (3) can easily be expressed in the form of IF . . . THEN statements:

2) IF the distance between the current city (A) and another city (B) is less than that between (A) and each of the other cities, THEN go to (B).
3) IF there are still unvisited cities on the list, THEN repeat step (2).

With this method, the computer has only to examine the path to each remaining city at each choice point. With 80 cities, the problem now becomes reasonable. From the starting city, the computer examines the 79 possibilities and goes to the nearest city. From there, it looks at the remaining 78 cities and goes to the nearest, and so forth. It can solve the problem quite quickly, and the answer it reaches will be close to the best possible route.

Any-Path Problems

While the traveling salesman problem is much simpler than the AI problems of today, it provides a good illustration of the use of an algorithm. There are many other "best-path problems," in which the object is to choose the best way to a solution. But in some situations, it is not necessary to choose the best path; any path will do, as long as a solution is reached. For efficiency's sake, the method should solve the problem in as few steps as possible, but taking a roundabout route is acceptable. In order to speed things up, ways to limit the search are also incorporated into the program.

The Water Jug Problem

Here is an example of an any-path problem: You are given two jugs. One holds four gallons, the other, three. Neither jug has any measuring marks on it. How can you use these two jugs to get exactly two gallons in the four gallon jug? For a computer to reach a solution, the problem must be turned into symbols that a computer can understand. This is called the "representational problem" in AI. There may be many different ways to represent a problem, and choosing a good one is a key factor to the success or failure of a program. The water jug problem is easily represented by using pairs of numbers. The number of gallons of water in the two jugs can be placed within parentheses, with the gallons in the four-gallon jug indicated first and those in the three-gallon jug second. Thus, the starting state is (0,0)—no water in either jug—while the desired state is (2,n)—two gallons in the four-gallon jug. "N" can be any number from 0 to 3, since it doesn't matter how many gallons are in the three-gallon jug at the end. Now we can start filling the jugs and pouring water from one into the other in all possible ways:

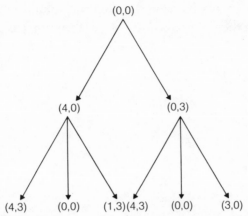

As you can see, it doesn't take long before the number of alternatives gets large. How can we limit the search of possible paths to a solution? One way is to have the program check back at each step to see if a previous state has been duplicated. In the last line, two procedures have resulted in both jugs being empty, which was the starting state. Exploring this alternative further will get us nowhere with the problem. The program can also check to see if any alternatives at each level are identical. With this problem, these simple checks cut the alternative paths at step 3 in half:

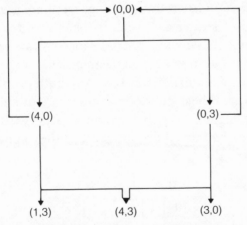

Checking for duplication greatly enhances the speed and efficiency of the program. This technique is vital in AI programming, where mind-boggling numbers of alternatives are commonplace. By the way, the eventual solution to the problem comes from the right-hand side of the diagram, called the "search tree":

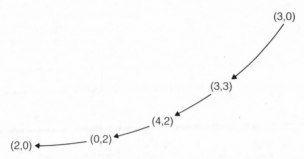

Strategies for Solving Problems

Every problem requires an effective strategy for reaching a solution. A program that uses a search tree explores the alternatives at each choice point, called a "node," and follows them until it finds a solution. The difficulty with trees is that, as we have seen, they tend to get very large very fast. The water jug tree was limited by checking back at each level for nonfruitful branches and eliminating them. This strategy is called "pruning the search tree." Generally speaking, trees are very inefficient unless "control strategies," such as heuristics for limiting the number of branches explored, can be incorporated into the programs to keep the trees of manageable size.

Other strategies work better with any-path problems such as the familiar hand-held puzzle with numbers of sliding tiles. In this example, eight tiles are present on a puzzle with nine spaces. The tiles must be moved around so that they appear in a particular numerical order:

(1)

2	8	3
1	6	4
7		5

Initial State

(2)

1	2	3
8		4
7	6	5

Goal State

The puzzle can be mathematically represented much as it looks to the eye—as a matrix of nine numbers, three across and three down. There are many different states into which the tiles and the blank space can be arranged—362,880 to be exact, or 9! Getting from the initial state (1) to the goal state (2) requires a number of moves. What is the best way to represent them? Each of the eight tiles can be moved in one of four directions— up, down, left, right. We could write the problem to include 32 (eight tiles times four directions) possible rules, one for each move of a numbered tile. The rules could only be applied when one of the tiles in question was next to the blank space.

There is a simpler way to specify the moves, however. If we make rules for shifting the BLANK space, then we reduce the number of rules from 32 to only four—move the blank left, right, up, or down. When the blank is adjacent to the side of the puzzle, even fewer than four moves will be possible—two or three, depending on whether it is in the corner or not. This example clearly shows the importance of designing a simple but accurate representation for a problem.

Now the rules for moving the blank space must be carefully spelled out. First of all, the program must specify that the blank can only shift into a space currently occupied by a number; that will keep it from moving out of the matrix. Next, we need rules for when to keep following a particular path, how to identify a path that won't be fruitful, and how to recognize the ultimate goal state. We might program the computer, for example, to interrupt a random pattern of movement when the sum of three tiles in the top row equals six. At this point, the program could move the space around only in the top two rows until the sequence 1, 2, 3 was reached. Then it could be told to leave the top row alone and work until another criterion for one of the other rows was satisfied.

We also need to decide on a strategy. Instead of utilizing a search tree, we will employ another powerful AI technique called "backtracking." In a complex problem, it may be necessary to tell the computer to investigate one path at a time instead of exploring a tree. But when a large number of sequential moves

Opposite page: Using backtracking to solve the 8-puzzle. The blank space is randomly moved until either (1) a previous arrangement of the numbers is duplicated, or (2) six moves have been made without reaching the preliminary goal of having the numbers in the top row add up to 6.

In column A, the blank is randomly moved from the starting state until a previous state is duplicated (5A is the same as 3A). The program backtracks to state 4 and continues to move the blank (column B). State 6B duplicates 4A, so the program again backtracks to the previous state—5B. In column C, the sixth move does not lead to a solution, and all possible rules on how to move the blank have already been applied to state 5. Therefore, the program backtracks to state 4 and moves the blank randomly. In column D, six moves have again been applied without reaching a goal state, so the program would again backtrack. Since all possible moves have been applied to state 4, the program would now backtrack to state 3 and try again.

As you can see, backtracking is not a very efficient way to solve the 8-puzzle. When purely random moves are used, a great deal of time can be wasted in reaching the goal state.

may be involved, a great deal of time could be wasted recovering from mistakes. The program must detect errors as early as possible and have rules for when to backtrack. This way, if the application of a particular rule isn't getting anywhere, the program can go back to a previous choice point and try another rule.

With the 8-puzzle, we can give the following rules and see what happens: (1) Back up when the arrangement of numbers is the same as at a previous step (this is similar to the rule applied in the water jug problem); (2) Back up when a set number of rules have been applied without reaching a preliminary goal, such as the top line adding up to 6. Let us say we have programmed the computer to back up when it has made six moves (applied six rules) and not reached the preliminary goal. The computer randomly moves the blank space around, backtracking when it encounters the conditons of rules (1) and (2).

Hill-Climbing

The computer could take a long time to solve the 8-puzzle using a trial-and-error method such as that outlined above. If we apply

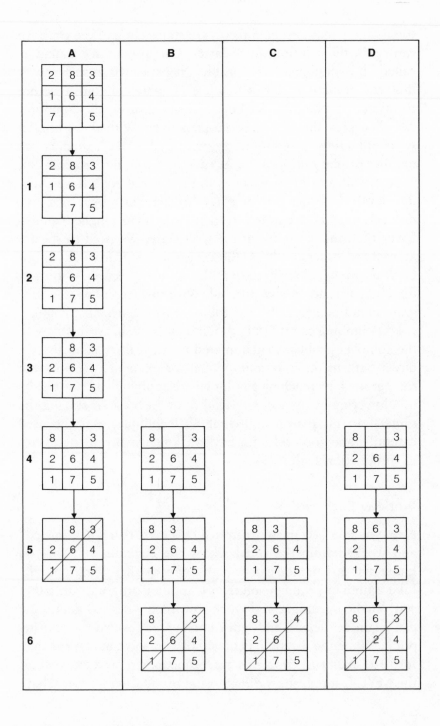

some other rules that help recognize states close to the goal, we can reach the solution much faster. One productive stategy is called "hill-climbing." The problem is presented in such a way that the computer can evaluate each potential move before choosing a path. After looking over its choices, the computer can then pick the best possible maneuver. With the 8-puzzle, we could tell the program to try, with each move, to reduce the number of tiles out of place. At each position, the program can compare all possible new states to the desired goal. If we show the number of tiles out of place in each state by a negative number, then the program can try to "climb" to a higher value— fewer tiles out of place—at the next state. We need to specify at least one other condition, however—if a higher value cannot be reached by moving the blank in any direction, choose a direction at random and proceed. With this technique, the program could quickly solve the 8-puzzle (see figure next page).

Hill-climbing can result in difficulties, though, especially with the complex problems encountered in AI. If there is no simple, direct path to the maximum value, for example, the program can get stuck by reaching a point where applying any rule results in a lowering of the value instead of an increase or staying the same. For this reason, hill-climbing techniques must be used carefully, and good rules for backtracking usually are necessary in conjunction with them.

Working Backward

Have you ever become so frustrated by a maze that you "cheated" and worked from the end back to the beginning? If so, you know that this method can be highly effective in solving a puzzle. Like a human problem-solver, a computer program can either start at the beginning and work toward the desired goal, or it can begin at the end and work backwards toward the starting point. While the 8-puzzle is no simpler to solve backward than forward, many AI problems are. Some expert systems, such as the MYCIN program for diagnosing blood diseases (see Chapter 7), employ this technique. Sometimes the most fruitful way to solve a problem is to work from both ends at the same time, simultaneously beginning at the start and at the finish. When the program works from the beginning toward the end, it is called "forward chaining." Working backwards is called "backward chaining."

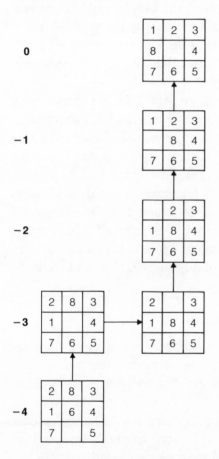

An effective way to solve the 8-puzzle is by using hill-climbing. A value of −1 is assigned for each tile not in the goal state at each move, and the computer is instructed to work its way upward until a value of zero, meaning all tiles are in place, is reached. Using this method, the computer can quickly reach the goal state.

How Do Humans Solve Problems?

One version of the tile-moving puzzle sold in stores has 16 squares with 15 numbered tiles. Because of the combinatorial explosion, this puzzle sold to humans is too difficult for the computer. For example, there are 15! arrangements of the tiles with the blank space in the lower right-hand corner of the puzzle, and 16! different states into which the blank could be moved. Current computers cannot deal with that many possibilities at once, but the human mind has been known to untangle this puzzle—so there must be heuristics that work. The trick is in figuring out what they are.

Herbert A. Simon and others at MIT have compared how experts and novices solve complex problems and discovered that they use different methods. While the novices bring into play heuristics similar to those of current AI programs, carefully working out a problem step by step, the experts look at a problem as an entity and solve it by intuition rather than through logic and reason. Since getting a computer to solve a program using logic and reasoning like a novice human is still challenging, the day when we can program an "intelligent" computer to apply the intuitive techniques of a human expert is likely to lie sometime in the future.

AI Heuristics

While the examples used in this chapter are simpler than the subject matter of AI today, they have demonstrated some of the essentials for solving AI problems. We will learn more about problem-solving methods in later chapters, but the basic requirements for any AI program are identical. The knowledge needed in solving the problem has to be effectively represented, and an efficient search method must be employed.

Rigid algorithms cannot be used in the majority of AI problems. Here AI differs fundamentally from other computer programming. Computers are at their best when given specific rules that take advantage of the binary nature of their circuitry. Computers can run through large numbers of alternatives in systematic fashion, whereas the human mind can easily get confused when there are many choices. Our minds, however, can find flexible ways to restrict the range of possibilities, whereas a computer has to be given specific instructions for limiting searches. For this reason, certain types of AI programs, such as those that play chess (Chapter 8), tend to get only so far because of the consequences of the combinatorial explosion. They are also stuck because, despite the ever larger memories of computers, the human mind still contains far more information than even the "smartest" computer. A chess Master, for example, has about 50,000 alternatives—the equivalent of computer "IF . . . THEN" statements—stored in his or her mind about how to play the game. One chess-playing computer program, the Cray Blitz, has that many programmed moves. While that program is within striking distance of Master status, its heuristics may not be as efficient as the chess Master's mind.

The most successful applications of computers so far involve "number crunching"—manipulation of large quantities of binary numbers with great rapidity and accuracy. Even functions such as word processing, which appear on the surface to involve something other than numbers, are really just variations on manipulating numbers. As we learned in Chapter 2, each letter of the alphabet and punctuation mark is represented in the computer by a unique byte, a sequence of eight zeros and ones in the computer's binary code. Word processing requires nothing more than manipulating the bytes that represent letters and punctuation marks according to absolute rules set down in the word processing program.

AI requires the manipulation of symbols instead of numbers. The meaning of a word is what counts in AI, not the sequence of letters that represent it. Because word meaning varies, depending on context, an AI program must use flexible heuristics that refer to stored information about the context of words. It must contain ways to limit searches to avoid the combinatorial explosion encountered in even the simplest programs involving the real world. There are many computer languages, but only a few possess the features necessary for AI.

5

Languages for Artificial Intelligence

The "native tongue" of all computers is some form of "machine language," the sequences of ones and zeros discussed in Chapter 2. Machine language is easy for computers but extremely difficult for people, so people have developed other programming languages that allow them to communicate more easily with computers. There are already about 200 different programming languages, with new ones on the way. Some languages, such as BASIC (Beginners' All-purpose Symbolic Instruction Code) and Pascal (named after the great seventeenth-century French mathematician Blaise Pascal) are meant to be relatively easy to learn and flexible. Others meet more specific needs—FORTRAN (FORmula TRANslator) was designed for solving mathematical, engineering, and science problems (though it is also used in business), while COBOL (COmmon Business-Oriented Language) was developed for business applications. Each language has its own strong points and weaknesses. But all of them, before actually being implemented, must be translated into machine language code by the computer itself.

A single instruction in a "high level language"—one that is far removed from machine code—may replace dozens of machine language instructions.

Some languages came into being because of AI. An AI language needs several special capabilities. First of all, it must be able to deal easily with words as symbols of meaning, not just as strings of characters. It must be flexible. Since AI involves a variety of types of information, different parts of the program must be able to interact to make it effective. Because backtracking and searching are such vital aspects of AI, the language must also be easily programmed to repeat the same series of steps over and over again, using different data each time. And finally, a language that allows programs to be put together one piece at a time enables a programmer to try out or test his or her creations section by section. This trait is especially important for an AI language because of the length and complexity of the programs.

Like other computer programming, artificial intelligence relies more on some languages than on others. In the United States, LISP (for LISt Processing) is the most popular AI tongue, while PROLOG (for PROgramming in LOGic), developed to facilitate logic programming, is more commonly used in Europe. The Japanese are employing modifications of PROLOG in their massive "Fifth Generation" push toward intelligent machines (see Chapter 13). While not often used in serious AI programming, LOGO (from the Greek word for "word" or "thought") has many of the same useful characteristics as LISP. A few other languages, such as the relatively new Smalltalk, also hold promise for AI applications.

LISP

LISP was one of the first computer languages. John McCarthy designed it back in the late 1950's, when computer science was in its infancy. FORTRAN and COBOL, also developed then, have fallen out of favor with computer scientists, but LISP has gained in strength with the rise of AI and has been modified into different "dialects."

In many computer languages, data can be presented in a variety of forms. But in LISP, the only data structure is a list. LISP lists have two advantages over the data structures in most computer languages. BASIC, for example, uses data structures called arrays to store data. A BASIC array must be set at a certain size. Lists, however, have no size limit, so they can be easily modified and expanded. In addition, a list can contain numbers, symbols, variables, words, strings of words, and other lists. Arrays are restricted to numbers or strings of a fixed number of characters. Thus lists are especially flexible in the kinds of information they can hold.

A LISP list is shown as a group of elements enclosed in parentheses: (THIS IS A LIST) is a list consisting of four elements—the symbols THIS, IS, A, and LIST. (THIS IS (A LIST WITH THREE ELEMENTS)) is also a list. The three elements are THIS, IS, and the list (A LIST WITH THREE ELEMENTS), which has five elements. A LISP program itself is nothing more than a list. And since a list can contain other lists, a LISP program that controls other programs is easy to write. The other program is simply included as one of the lists, along with the circumstances under which the program is to be implemented.

A LISP program can quickly become an eye-straining tangle, with lists within lists within lists, all marked off by parentheses. But once you begin to interpret the program, starting with the innermost parentheses and working outward, it all makes sense. For example, an arithmetic problem that looks simple in BASIC comes out quite differently in LISP. The BASIC expression $C - 2 * A + 5/B$ (in computer programs, multiplication is usually indicated by using "*") is programmed in LISP as $(- C (+ (* 2 A)(/ 5 B)))$. To understand the BASIC statement, you need to know the rules of precedence for carrying out arithmetic functions. But the LISP program specifies the order within the framework of the lists. Notice also that, in LISP, the functions, such as "$-$" or "*" are placed as the first elements in the list. This is true for words as well as numbers. To make a list of "bread, wine, and cheese," you would need to write (and bread wine cheese). At first this seems strange, but once it becomes familiar, understanding the purpose of the list in the program is easy.

Like many other programming languages, LISP has some predefined functions. When one of these is at the beginning of a list, the computer applies that function to the list. With a couple of LISP functions, IF . . . THEN statements are easy to program. Here is a simple conditional statement in LISP:

```
(cond ((eq y 1) 'land)
      ((eq y 2) 'sea))
```

This is LISP's version of how Paul Revere should interpret "One if by land, two if by sea."

In LISP, the function "cond" tells the computer to check the lists that follow—called "conditional clauses"—to see if one of them is true. In this case, there are two conditional clauses. The function "eq" is used to check the truth of a statement. Following "eq" are two elements—"y" and "1" in the first conditional clause, "y" and "2" in the second. If y = 1, the first conditional clause is true; if y = 2, the second one is. Once the computer finds a conditional clause that is true, it produces the result, which is the last element in the list—"land" or "sea." Thus, if we told the computer that y = 2, it would check the conditional statement. Since y is not 1, it would pass over the first conditional clause. When it came to the second one, it would see that the two elements following "eq" are the same—y = 2—so it would go on to give the result of that conditional clause, "sea," as the answer. Notice that the second conditional clause was written below the first. For clarity, LISP programmers prefer to write their programs this way, rather than stringing them out in a long sequence of symbols.

PROLOG

PROLOG was invented about 1970 in France. It has been used extensively in Europe ever since, but Americans have not seri-

ously explored its potential until recently. With its logic ori-
entation, it applies to certain kinds of problems involving thought,
since much thought is based on logical deduction. For example,
a classic syllogism (a form of reasoning in which a logical conclusion is made from two factual statements) is the following:

Socrates is a man.
All men are mortal.
Therefore, Socrates is mortal.

The first two statements are facts, the third is the conclusion
that can be drawn from these facts. Here are the first two statements translated into PROLOG, with "human" substituted for
"man" to make it more general:

human (socrates)
mortal (Something):-human (Something)

The first PROLOG line is easy to understand; it states simply
that Socrates is human. The second statement is a bit more
complicated, for it involves variables, or functions that can have
a number of different values. For example, in the arithmetic
statement, $Y = X + 3$, Y is a function of X; that is, as X
changes, so does Y. The statement "All men are mortal" does
not specify a particular man; it says *all* men. Therefore we know
that anything designated as a man will also be mortal. Notice
that in PROLOG, the name "Socrates" is not capitalized. Cap-
itals are reserved for variables. Socrates is a constant, since he
is a particular man. In the second line, Something is a variable.
The PROLOG statement says, in effect, "If you want to find
something mortal, look for something human." We have now
created a PROLOG "rule." We can give the above rule to a
computer with PROLOG and ask it the following:

mortal (Who)

The computer will now search through its rules to find any that
govern the state of being mortal. Notice that "Who" is a vari-

able; PROLOG will search for all values for that variable by examining its rules. When it finds the rule that anything identified as human is also mortal, and then comes across the statement that socrates is a human, it will give this result:

Who = socrates

It has given the value, socrates, to the variable, Who.

Notice that this result could also be represented in the form of IF . . . THEN statements, which, as we have seen, are a key part of many AI programs:

IF Socrates is a man, and IF all men are mortal, THEN Socrates is mortal.

Because IF . . . THEN statements are basic to its structure, PROLOG is very useful for AI work.

Contrasting PROLOG and LISP

PROLOG and LISP both have advantages and disadvantages for AI work. American expert systems such as MYCIN are written in LISP. But some workers, such as Ross Overbeek of the Argonne National Laboratory in Argonne, Illinois, think that PROLOG or other logic-based languages would be more effective for expert systems. While the rules for diagnosing diseases can be phrased in LISP using conditional statements, they also can be easily stated in PROLOG. When a program is written in LISP, the computer runs through the statements in the order they are written and executes each instruction in sequence. With PROLOG, however, the rules are scanned to find those that apply, no matter where they are located in the program. Rules that don't apply are passed over, and no unnecessary work is done by the program. This makes PROLOG potentially more efficient. Also, two important features of AI programs—searching and backtracking—are built into PROLOG, but must be programmed specifically into LISP routines.

The most serious problem with the rigidly logical basis of PROLOG is that you can't say "I don't know." If something can't be proven, it is assumed to be false. In AI, propositions concerning unknowns often come up, creating difficulties for PROLOG. With LISP, however, it is easy to insert an extra clause to a conditional statement that will tell the computer what to do if none of the other conditions are met.

Alan Robinson of Syracuse University has developed a new language called LOGLISP that takes advantage of the strengths of both PROLOG and LISP. It combines the programming ease of LISP with the advantages of logic. LOGLISP is, however, just a beginning. Robinson and his co-workers are now developing a new, single language that is not a hybrid of existing languages. This language will allow programming both with functions (like LISP), which are very powerful tools, and with logic (like PROLOG). They want this language to be such a natural combination of the two approaches that users don't feel they are dealing with two different methods that have been artifically merged.

LOGO

LOGO was developed at the MIT Artificial Intelligence Laboratory by Seymour Papert and his colleagues as a language for helping children develop problem-solving skills. LOGO can be learned naturally, through active participation, which helps develop logical thinking. One thing that makes LOGO different from LISP and PROLOG is its powerful graphics capability. It uses a device called a "turtle" to produce graphic images. The original turtle was a mechanical object that moved across the floor and drew with a pen or paper. It was commanded from the computer. Today, the turtle has been reduced to a pointer on the monitor screen, and it can do some fancy artwork. The LOGO turtle is so useful that it has been adapted to other languages such as Smalltalk and Pascal. In addition to turtle graphics, LOGO has list-processing capabilities, making it a good candidate for AI programming.

A LOGO program can be built up piece by piece by writing small routines that can be incorporated into larger routines and

Seymour Papert and two children work with one of the original MIT turtles. The symbolic turtle on the screen in LOGO represents this machine, which moved across the floor under the command of a computer running LOGO.
The MIT Museum.

programs. Let's use a graphics example to show how this is done. A house can easily be built up of smaller parts—for a simple house, the lower part of the house and the roof. LOGO commands tell the turtle which direction to move and what angle to turn. When a number follows the commands "forward" or "backward," it refers to the number of "steps" the turtle should move. When numbers follow "right" or "left," they indicate the number of degrees the turtle should turn. Here is a LOGO routine for making a square of a particular size:

```
TO SQUARE
REPEAT 4 [FORWARD 50 RIGHT 90]
END
```

The first line tells LOGO that we are defining a procedure called "SQUARE." In the second line, we tell the turtle to go forward

50 steps, turn right 90 degrees, and repeat that procedure 4 times. This will draw a square on the screen. Note that LOGO uses brackets to set off lists instead of parentheses. Now, any time we want a square 50 units on a side, all we have to do is to type in the command:

SQUARE

The turtle will then draw the square.

We can modify this procedure by making the distance the turtle moves forward into a variable. Then we can draw squares of different sizes:

```
TO SQUARE :SIDE
REPEAT 4 [FORWARD :SIDE RIGHT 90]
END
```

The ":" indicates to LOGO that the word following will be a variable. Now we can draw squares of different sizes by telling the computer to square and following the command with a number:

```
SQUARE 50
or
SQUARE 10
```

For the roof, we can easily write a routine for drawing a triangle:

```
TO TRIANGLE :SIDE
REPEAT 3 [FORWARD :SIDE RIGHT 120]
END
```

This routine will draw an equilateral triangle. Notice that the turtle must turn 120° between sides, for it is turning outwards around the triangle, not inwards. By turning 120°, the turtle will produce the correct 60° internal angles for the triangle. Now, making a house is easy. All we have to do is define a new procedure using our defined procedures:

```
TO HOUSE :SIDE
SQUARE :SIDE
FORWARD :SIDE
RIGHT 60
TRIANGLE :SIDE
END
```

Notice that we have to tell the turtle to trace over the first side of the house to reach the upper left-hand corner of the house. Then it must turn 60° to the right to get it pointing the right direction to make the roof. Now, any time we want to draw a house, all we need to do is command the turtle:

HOUSE 50
or
HOUSE 25

We will get a house of the size we want.

LOGO Makes a House

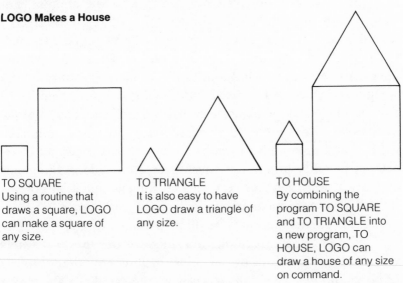

TO SQUARE
Using a routine that draws a square, LOGO can make a square of any size.

TO TRIANGLE
It is also easy to have LOGO draw a triangle of any size.

TO HOUSE
By combining the program TO SQUARE and TO TRIANGLE into a new program, TO HOUSE, LOGO can draw a house of any size on command.

The house we made here is very simple. It could also be made in the shape of a rectangle or with windows, for example. But however we defined it, once we told the turtle how to make a house, we would need only the single command to draw the house.

The same techniques we used here with graphics can also be used in LOGO with words. A LOGO program can be built up slowly, and each routine can easily be checked as the program gets more complex. Debugging the program—finding errors and fixing them—can be done along the way, making errors easy to find. In addition to having lists and variables, LOGO has conditionals such as IFTRUE and IFFALSE that are valuable for AI.

Smalltalk

The focus of this relatively new language is very different from that of LISP or PROLOG. LISP uses functions, PROLOG emphasizes logic, but Smalltalk is "object oriented." Everything in Smalltalk is an object. An object need not be an actual physical object; it can be a package of information. Smalltalk programs function by having objects send messages to one another. For example, in the arithmetic problem "5 + 2," the number 5 would send a message to the number 2—"add yourself to me."

Being object oriented makes Smalltalk a natural for writing adventure games, which feature objects such as monsters and weapons, castles and caves. Every Smalltalk object belongs to a particular class of objects, each of which can have unique attributes. In the monster class, for example, there might be goblins and gremlins. All monsters would share certain characteristics—they attack the adventurer, they hide in dungeons and caves, and they are very strong, for example. All goblins would have additional traits not shared with other kinds of monsters. There could also be different kinds of goblins—blue and red goblins, for example, that might differ in key ways as well. The specifications of the object include how that object is to be manipulated when it receives a message. Let's say that a goblin responds to an encounter with the adventurer by hitting him with a club, while a dragon reacts by breathing fire on him. The same message—that an adventurer was there—would therefore elicit different results from the two types of monsters.

One trait of Smalltalk that makes it promising for AI is its hierarchical arrangement—there are major classes, like monsters and weapons, each with subclasses, such as goblins and swords.

One of the first programs with overlapping windows was written at the Xerox Alto Research Center, using the powerful LISP dialog, Interlisp-D.
Courtesy Xerox Corporation.

The subclasses can be further divided. The hierarchies exhibit "inheritance"—that is, while goblins may have their own unique traits, they also share certain traits with all other monsters. Anything in the monster class automatically exhibits all the traits of monsters. Inheritance is a very important characteristic for programs such as expert systems and frame-based systems (see Chapter 6) as well as games. An advantage Smalltalk shares with LISP and LOGO is that programs can be written in smaller units. This allows for easy debugging and step-by-step building up of complex programs.

Smalltalk is easy to learn, too, because it uses a window interface like that of the Apple Macintosh computer. The window system originated with Xerox, which developed Smalltalk and from which Apple borrowed it. Windows are very useful, for they allow a programmer to keep different aspects of the work on the screen at the same time as a series of overlapping "pages," like papers on a desk.

Languages of the Future

No one language is "perfect" for any application. As AI becomes more sophisticated and varied, different dialects or entire languages will be developed to meet new specialized needs.

The Japanese Fifth Generation project (see Chapter 13) has already resulted in one modified version of PROLOG, and more will follow. Add to this the new logic and function language being developed at Syracuse University, and there will be at least two new AI languages in the near future. And as computers with parallel processors are perfected (see Chapter 13), new languages will be needed to handle the expanded capabilities of the new machines.

6

Programming for True Language Understanding

Wrestling with the complexities of natural language understanding by computers may help us comprehend the essence of human language and thought. Many AI researchers are at least as interested in uncovering the workings of the mind as they are in developing computer programs. In this quest, the problems of how we understand language and how we organize and access the commonsense knowledge in our memories are intimately intertwined.

There are two basic views among AI scientists as to how the mind might organize information, each originally put forth by a different founder of AI, John McCarthy, now of Stanford University, and Marvin Minsky of MIT.

Frames

Minsky believes that the mind arranges its own knowledge around structures he calls "frames." A frame represents a particular stereotyped situation—eating in a restaurant, for example. When a person enters a restaurant, he or she knows from experience

Marvin Minsky, one of the founders of AI, is shown here in the early days of robots, watching an MIT model (which he helped develop) at work in its blocks world.
The MIT Museum.

what to do and what to expect. Certain things are true about any restaurant—we go there to eat, we will look at a menu, and so on. The top levels of a frame contain the things that are always true about a particular situation. Below the top levels are lower levels with slots, which Minsky calls "terminals," that can be filled by specific information. Related frames are linked together as "frame systems," and a given frame can have subframes. For example, the "fast-food" restaurant subframe would include information that would include information that one goes up to a counter to order rather than sitting down at a table. The restaurant frame itself, on the other hand, might be one frame of an "eating" frame system.

One crucial point of Minsky's idea is that all of the terminals in a frame have what he calls "default" settings. For example, if someone tells you, "John kicked the ball," you will imagine a particular ball, depending on your own experience. You might picture a football, while another person may envision a soccer ball. If a particular type of ball is specified, you don't need to extract the particular ball you have in the default setting in your own mind. This is an interesting way of explaining the observation discussed in Chapter 3 that people will interpret the same words in very different ways. To one person, "tall doctor" invokes a wise and caring healer, while to another, it brings to mind an intimidating and stern authority figure. Minsky would say that these two people had different default settings at the terminal for "tall doctor."

E. Charniak, in his Ph.D work at MIT, studied how children understand stories, even when very little information about the situation is given. The following story leaves out a great deal, yet we easily understand what is going on, and so would a child:

> Jane was invited to Jack's birthday party.
> She wondered if he would like a kite.
> She went to her room and shook her piggy bank.
> It made no sound.

The word "present" is never mentioned, yet we know that Jane is thinking about what to give Jack. When a birthday party is mentioned, Minsky would say that our minds call up the birthday party frame. We know that we are expected to give a present when invited to a party. The word "present" is suggested by the second line. We know that presents cost money, so we understand why Jane went to her piggy bank, even though money is never mentioned. We also know that when a piggy bank makes no sound, it is empty, so we understand Jane's dilemma all too well! While the idea of frames helps us see why this story can be understood despite its lack of detail, we still do not know just how the chains of association among the words and ideas are linked in the mind.

The Logic Approach

McCarthy believes that AI programs should use a logical structure. He feels that frames won't do the job, because the frame always dominates the situation. McCarthy thinks that a variety of different sources interact in comprehending a given situation; there isn't always one dominating frame. With frames, the terminals cannot interact directly with one another. McCarthy views this as a serious flaw of the frame idea. He thinks that units which are more interactive than the terminals of frames would come closer to representing the way our minds really work.

There are difficulties with ordinary logic, however. If you make a statement such as "Birds can fly" and follow it with "The ostrich is a bird," the logical deduction is that "Ostriches can fly." Formal "monotonic" logic doesn't allow for exceptions such as flightless birds. Our minds clearly do not work this rigidly; we are able to take into account exceptions. McCarthy proposes using a modified form of logic, a "nonmonotonic" type, that would allow for ambiguity. For example, with non-monotonic logic, you could say, "The boat may be used as a vehicle for crossing a body of water unless something prevents it." This could not be done with traditional logic; every possible exception would have to be individually described. But with McCarthy's method, as long as there was no stated condition preventing use of the boat, the assumption that the boat could be used to cross water would be allowed. If a phrase such as "leak in the boat" were present, the program would go off on a new path dealing with leaks, water, and repair. Here, instead of a dominating frame (as in Minsky's model) there is a chain of interrelated logical statements without a dominant theme.

Another way around the absolutism of classical logic is "fuzzy logic," developed by mathematician Lofti A. Zadeh of the University of California, Berkeley. With ordinary logic, objects and concepts must be placed in categories with clear borders; with fuzzy logic, the boundaries can be indistinct. Fuzzy logic allows degrees of states such as length. A board could be *very* short, or *somewhat* long, instead of just short or long. Even with such qualifiers, it is possible, using fuzzy logic, to translate natural language into mathematically derived computer code. Fuzzy logic has already been used to create a backgammon program that beat the world champion, and to design a system for controlling the operation of the complex industrial processes of steam engines and kilns, which involve continuous variables such as temperature.

Will Either Method Work?

Minsky and McCarthy criticize each other's approaches to natural language programming. McCarthy thinks frames won't succeed because they don't allow enough interaction among the individual units of information. McCarthy points out that scientists such as Roger Schank (see later in this chapter), who are writing programs based on frames, are finding out that they need interacting packets of information in order to get their programs to work. This is a move in the direction of logic.

Minsky, on the other hand, doesn't think logic is flexible enough to express how we think. In his view, all our thought patterns cannot be characterized as logical, and the problem of how to organize many small, independently true propositions so that they can be properly accessed is too great. We need ways of linking the pieces of knowledge to the rules about how they are used.

Douglas Lenat of Stanford expresses another concern about using logic in programming:

The power of logical methods lies in their representation of the world in symbols that can be manipulated in well-understood ways . . . to produce inferences. That power is also their greatest weakness: many types of knowledge, including the uncertain and incomplete knowledge characteristic of most real-world problems, do not lend themselves to representation through precise logical formalisms. Programs that draw exclusively on logic are capturing only part of the understanding an intelligent person would bring to bear in attempting to solve a difficult problem.

In truth, neither logic nor the concept frames has yet proved practical in producing intelligent programs. Roger Schank and his followers use modifications of the frame approach and have made important contributions to AI. But, like all AI programs so far, theirs have only limited spheres of knowledge and are far from foolproof. Neither Minsky nor McCarthy believes that computers will soon reach anything near the human level of intelligence, but their belief doesn't stop others from trying. We will return to the problem of organizing knowledge in Chapter 12.

Natural Language Understanding and the Mind

By trying to get computers to interpret words as people do, AI researchers hope to discover basic truths about the nature of human language. Languages vary greatly in structure. Related languages, such as German and English, share many common points of grammar and vocabulary, while unrelated ones, like English and Japanese, are very dissimilar. Some people believe, however, that there is a basic core shared by all human languages, a deep grammatical structure that is universal. If so, and if that core can be discovered, then we will have learned some profound truths about the human mind.

The discovery of a shared deep structure among languages would also make natural language understanding by computers much easier and would allow the techniques developed for use with one language to be applied easily to others. Many researchers believe that only by figuring out how people go about understanding language will we be able to get computers to do so. After all, the successes in AI so far have been in areas where we have some idea of the way the mind handles the subject. In game programs, the computer examines a number of possible moves and evaluates them before making its move. Good human chess players probably choose moves in much the same way. Great players, however, almost certainly use additional techniques that have yet to be duplicated by the computer. Even with programming on bigger and faster computers, a machine program may never equal a human chess Grand Master until we can unravel the way a Grand Master's mind works. Expert systems are successful because they were written in consultation with human experts who could communicate to computer scientists how they go about making decisions. Maybe we will succeed with natural language understanding only when we figure out how people achieve it.

Translating Languages

The idea of using computers to translate from one natural language to another has been around since the beginning of the computer age. At first, researchers hoped that the same techniques used to crack secret military codes could translate natural languages. It wasn't long, however, before completely unintelligible "translations" showed that the problem was a tough one. Here, one must deal in two languages with all the problems of ambiguity, shared knowledge, idioms, and so on. Idioms are a particular stumbling block. Even humans can have trouble translating idioms, as in the famous silent pause of the English-Russian translator at the United Nations who didn't know how to render into Russian U.S. Ambassador Adlai Stevenson's 1962 pronouncement that we would keep missiles out of Cuba "until hell freezes over." Another story has a computer program taking the phrase, "Out of sight, out of mind," translating it into Russian, and then back into English as "invisible, insane."

Translating languages is also difficult because of differing grammar. For example, while most languages assign a gram-

"YOU CAN PUT AWAY YOUR TRANSLATING CALCULATOR NOW. I'M SPEAKING TO YOU IN ENGLISH."

Will computers ever get good enough at language translation to do our work for us?
Sidney Harris.

matical gender to each noun, English does not. In French or Spanish, every noun is either masculine or feminine, and there is a masculine and a feminine form for the words "the" and "a." Modern Greek has no infinitive form of the verb, and many languages have different kinds of verb tenses that do not translate easily into those of another tongue. All these differences create big problems for language translation.

Beyond Language

Perhaps the shared nature of human language is not at the level of grammar but is even deeper, at the level of concepts. Using this idea, Roger Schank of Yale University has developed a way of getting computers to interpret language. Schank calls his approach "conceptual dependency," because it emphasizes the relationships of basic concepts to one another. He gets around the ambiguity of language by representing two different sentences that have the same meaning in the same way. He reduces actions to eleven basic types and gives them names. "ATrans" is the term for all forms of taking, giving, and buying, while "PTrans" applies to any action resulting in the physical transfer of an object from one place to another—walking, putting, riding, and so on. The transfer of information is represented by "MTrans," which includes writing and talking. This system reduces all actions to their most basic level. The TV news MTrans the news to its viewers; the bank teller ATrans money to someone who cashes a check (ATrans is used here because possession of the money is changing from one person to another). The person can then PTrans himself to the store in his car to shop, and so forth.

Schank uses a modification of the frame idea to express how people organize knowledge. When a person encounters a familiar situation, Schank believes that a set of expectations, which he calls a "script," is called to mind. The fast-food script has similarities to and differences from the regular restaurant script. A script allows a person to anticipate the behavior of others and to know how he or she should behave as well. Schank has used the script idea to create programs that can analyze stories and can sometimes explain why people behave in certain ways in those stories.

Analyzing Language

The most successful natural language programs so far all deal with limited scenarios. As we already saw in Chapter 3, a natural language program must know a great deal about context in order to appear "intelligent." When the number of possible interpretations is limited by restricting the scenario, fewer definitions of the words are possible, and the program can more easily analyze and "understand" the material it is given.

First of all, the program sees how the words relate to one another grammatically. The part of the program that unravels the sentence structure or syntax, using the rules of grammar and other knowledge about the language, is called the "parser." For example, in the sentence "John hit the ball," the parser figures out that John carried out an action that affected the ball; "John" is the subject and "ball" is the object. The parser separates the parts of the sentence, dividing it up into appropriate fragments from which meaning can be deciphered.

Once the parser has taken apart the sentence, the program then proceeds to figure out the actual meaning of the string of words, or the "semantics." To unravel the semantics of a sentence, a program assigns meanings to the individual words. It needs clues about how to interpret words with several definitions. The word "diamond," for example, has some very different meanings. The computer could be told that the gemstone interpretation should be assumed when the rest of the sentence tags it as a transportable physical object—"Mary dropped her diamond." The word "dropped" specifies a physical object that can be moved from place to place. The playing field definition could be keyed as a location—"Let's play at the diamond on Saturday." Here the word "at" specifies a time or location. Such properties of word meanings are called "semantic markers"; they help indicate which meaning of the word is appropriate.

Unfortunately, the semantic marker approach can get tripped up. "Bill saw Mary's diamond glittering from across the room," for example, contains no clue as to whether the diamond involved is a movable physical object, a location, or a different type of thing altogether. To solve this dilemma, strings of adjectives and adverbs related to the different types of diamonds— "glittering," "shining," "sparkling," and so on—could be added. Even then, ambiguous sentences could still come along. "The park had a small diamond," for example, would be a puzzle for the computer unless "park" had been keyed in as yet another semantic marker for the baseball meaning. Sentences such as "The baseball player's wife had a big diamond" might crash the program—a wife has a gemstone diamond, but "baseball" would surely be a semantic marker for the playing field!

Once a natural language program has dissected the relationships of the words to one another and assigned a definition to each word, it must go back and reinterpret the sentence to get its meaning, taking into account everything it has established. The procedure for interpreting a sentence can be summarized as follows:

1) Figure out how the words relate to one another (the syntax).
2) Assign meanings to each of the words.
3) Interpret the meaning (semantics) of the sentence.

The process cannot always proceed in step-wise fashion, for the relationships of the words often can't be figured out without first knowing their appropriate meanings in the sentence. For example, interpreting "Mary went to the park with the tall tree" and "Mary went to the park with the tall stranger" requires knowing the meanings of the words "tree" and "stranger" before grammatical placement can be assigned to the word "with." One useful type of natural language system is a "conceptual analyzer" to derive meaning from sentences. Instead of first dissecting a sentence for syntax, the conceptual analyzer goes through it one word at a time, starting at the beginning and trying to relate each word to those already stored in its memory. In this way, a sentence can be unraveled without first taking it apart. If the conceptual analyzer runs into trouble and cannot figure out a sentence using this technique, it will fall back on syntax as a last resort.

SHRDLU

Because even limited real-world scenarios can sometimes be too complex to handle, AI researchers have often used artificial worlds, to make misinterpretation less likely. By succeeding with simple worlds, they hope to learn principles that apply to the real world.

Perhaps the best known of these programs is SHRDLU, developed by Terry Winograd (now at Stanford) as his 1972 Ph.D. work at MIT. SHRDLU (the letters apparently do not stand for anything) operates in a "blocks world," where blocks of different sizes, shapes, and colors lie on a tabletop. A robot arm can move the blocks around according to instructions given by a person. Winograd's blocks world doesn't actually exist on any real tabletop; it is shown as a picture on a display screen. Designing an actual robot arm and getting it to work would be a big project in itself.

When a person types in a command to the computer, SHRDLU answers back. If the command is understood, the computer answers "OK," and the arm on the screen carries out the task. If there is a problem, the computer asks for clarification. "Pick up the pyramid" might elicit the answer "I don't understand which pyramid you mean." The computer "knows" that the word "the" refers to a specific object, but there are three pyramids to choose from. SHRDLU understands fairly complex commands such as "Find a block that is taller than the one you are holding and put it into the box." This request requires the computer to note which block it is holding and examine the table to find a bigger one. Because it is not clear from the request what "it" refers to, the computer states, "By 'it' I assume you mean the block that is taller than the one I am holding." The

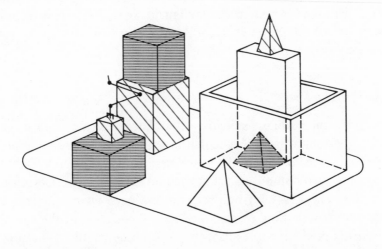

This is SHRDLU's imaginary tabletop with colored blocks. The image of this world is shown on the computer display screen. In addition to the blocks, there is a box from which SHRDLU can take blocks and into which it can put them. The imaginary robot arm that moves the blocks is shown attached to the small block in front. (Red blocks have diagonal lines, green blocks have horizontal lines, blue blocks have no lines).

computer can also remember the sequence of its moves and can answer questions such as "Did you move the red block before picking up the green pyramid?" It is also capable of limited learning. If the human operator says, "Pick up the pyramid on top of the house," the computer will reply, "Sorry, I don't know the word house." After the person types in "A house is a block with a pyramid on top," the computer will say "I understand," and the new word "house" will have been added to its vocabulary.

The SHRDLU system contains four basic parts—one to analyze grammar, another to recognize the grammatical components, one to convert the sentences into commands for the robot arm or into queries of its data base, and finally, one to solve the problems presented. If the computer was asked to put the blue block on the green one, the problem-solver part would know that it first had to remove any blocks that were on top of either the green or blue blocks before putting one on the other. Each of the system's four elements in turn contains several parts, all of which work smoothly together to perform in the blocks world Winograd designed.

The Turing Test

In 1950, the brilliant scientist Alan Turing wrote a paper so foresighted and insightful that it is still discussed today. When Turing wrote "Computing Machinery and Intelligence," only huge and slow computers using vacuum tubes were in operation. The first checkers-playing program had been written, but that was the closest thing to an "intelligent" program at the time.

Turing posed the question, "Can machines think?"—a question loaded with emotional content and problems of definition. Turing proposed a way to approach the question objectively. His method has become known as the "Turing Test." In the Turing Test, an interrogator communicates by way of a keyboard with another person and a machine, neither within sight range of the interrogator. The interrogator's goal would be to determine, by asking questions, whether subject A or subject B was the machine. The question then becomes: "If a machine could consistently fool human interrogators so they could not distinguish between the computer and the human, can the machine think?"

The Turing Test is a rigorous trial. The interrogator could ask any sort of question, and the computer would have to "figure out" how a human might answer it. If asked to write a poem about a particular subject, it would most likely have to find a way to get out of it by making the sort of response a human who didn't write poetry would make (Turing's example: COUNT ME OUT ON THIS ONE. I NEVER COULD WRITE POETRY). On the other hand, if confronted with a math problem, the computer would have to disguise its expertise. It could do this in a number of ways. It could wait for several seconds before giving a response. Then, if a problem was really hard, it might give a wrong answer. It could "pretend" not to be able to solve certain kinds of problems: I NEVER DID LEARN LONG DI-VISION.

Since there are no restrictions on the interrogator in the Turing Test, he or she could use slang expressions or specialized words that any contemporary human would understand, but which programmers could easily have not included in the program's vocabulary. The program would need to have, essentially, a complete vocabulary not only of basic word meanings but of all the slang expressions, old sayings, and so forth that we absorb as we grow up. Either that, or it would need a wide variety of clever responses to use when it didn't understand the questions.

The interrogator could also ask about any realm of human knowledge. As we have seen, the everyday pieces of detailed knowledge people take for granted are the hardest to recognize, enumerate, and program into computers. The answer to a simple question such as "Can you buy aspirin in the grocery store?" might give the computer away, as the programmer could easily have forgotten a small detail such as that aspirin, a drug, is so commonly used that it is available in grocery stores as well as drugstores.

Because of the vastness of knowledge possessed by every adult human being, a computer that could pass the Turing Test seems a thing of science fiction or the distant future—if indeed it could ever be produced. One reason SHRDLU is still discussed today with interest is that it is one of the few AI products that can carry on an "intelligent" conversation with a human. Go one step beyond the blocks world, however, and SHRDLU would be completely lost.

While a generalized intelligent machine may be impractical, specialized programs that behave "intelligently" in limited cir-cumstances can be very powerful and useful, as we will see in the next chapter.

7

Expert Systems

Imagine a country doctor far fom the city, baffled by the unusual illness of a young baby. If the doctor can't figure out what is wrong and fast, the baby will die. The doctor picks up the phone and dials a long distance number that connects her to a medical computer network. She rests the receiver in the cradle next to her computer and types the puzzling symptoms of her patient on the keyboard. After a pause, a couple of questions about the baby's condition appear on the screen, and the doctor answers them. Within moments, more words appear on the screen—the baby is suffering from a rare but treatable condition. The proper medication and its dosage are presented on the screen. The doctor hangs up and dials the nearest pharmacy immediately, ordering the lifesaving medicine for the infant.

Stories like this show the promise of expert systems, a promise they are not far from fulfilling. Within a few years, medical diagnosis systems will almost surely be on-line for any physicians who wish to take advantage of them, and they will save many lives. Expert systems are the one major practical result of AI research so far, and their use will become more and more common in many aspects of modern life besides medicine. They will help run complex factories, give financial advice, and carry out military operations.

While expert systems can't take the place of human judgment, they can be invaluable aids, with their own advantages. The knowledge of several human experts can sometimes be merged into one program. The programs can be updated with the latest knowledge, and they don't "forget" what they "know," even if they do not use certain parts of their memories for long periods of time. Computers don't get tired, suffer from stress, or panic under crisis conditions. Humans can keep only a few pieces of information comfortably in the conscious mind at one time; a computer doesn't suffer from such a limitation. And finally, expert systems can let the human experts concentrate their expertise on situations where they are most needed.

Unlike most of AI, expert systems have passed from the realm of experiment and conjecture into the real world. While the first of these complex programs took about 50 man years to design (a man year is the equivalent of one person working eight hours a day, five days a week, for one year), today it typically takes one to five man years to put such a system together. An expert system, designed by a specialist called a "knowledge engineer," can be developed to suit the needs of any buyer, as long as there is at least one expert willing and able to pinpoint how he or she makes decisions based on knowledge. Some companies in the computer industry specialize in expert systems, and there are even software packages for LISP computers that aid in designing expert systems.

Expert systems are often thought of as merely an offshoot to AI because their "intelligence" is arguable. They can be successful because they are limited in scope. Each system deals with only a narrow area of human knowledge and knows nothing outside of it. For example, MYCIN, developed at Stanford University by E. H. Shortliffe and others, is an expert system that can diagnose blood diseases and meningitis and recommend appropriate drug therapy. The program deals with diseases, tests, and symptoms, but it has no concept of what a patient, doctor, hospital, or death is. If you told MYCIN that you had taken its advice but that the patient died this morning, it would merely answer, INPUT UNGRAMMATICAL.

What They Can Do

Expert systems are valuable in many realms. Medical diagnosis is a particularly successful application. While MYCIN deals with blood infections, PUFF handles lung diseases, and ONCOCIN recommends therapy for cancer patients. Expert systems can also analyze malfunctions of machinery. They can take data given to them and predict what will come next, which is especially valuable to the military and to weather forecasters. They can monitor complex systems such as factories and can warn human operators of potential problems. By combining their abilities to diagnose, monitor, and predict, expert systems can be very helpful in difficult situations. A system called PICON (Process Intelligent CONtrol) can monitor 20,000 separate alarms and measurements in an oil refinery. The system runs on a LISP computer that communicates with the mainframe computer of the refinery, which in turn keeps track of the refinery's many sensors. If a problem arises, the mainframe passes the information to PICON, which evaluates it and reaches conclusions. If PICON needs more facts, it can ask the mainframe for data from other sensors. A human operator is informed of PICON's evaluations and makes final decisions.

Expert systems can be placed in control of factories or military operations. Computer-run assembly lines might not worry some people, but many people don't want machines to make the decisions about nuclear power plants or the military. In the film *War Games*, the human link in the military command is eliminated, leaving the computer completely in charge, with nearly disastrous consequences. No one wants this to happen in real life. Capabilities and control such as the computers have in *2001* and *2010* are also frightening to many people.

Expert systems can also act as designers. A system called R1, developed jointly by Digital Equipment Corporation (DEC) and

Carnegie-Mellon University, customizes VAX computer systems, a type popular with educational institutions and businesses, to meet the needs of different buyers. By interacting with engineers, expert systems can help design bug-free products such as computer chips. After a new chip is designed, the specifications are given to an expert system that checks to make sure the chip will function properly. The system can pinpoint problems and give the human designer tips on correcting them.

Many educators look forward to expert systems that embody the expertise of master teachers and can work with students suffering from learning disabilities. Such a program could test a student and look for consistent errors. Then it could assign problems and provide instruction specifically designed to help the student overcome his or her particular weaknesses. One big advantage of a computer in such a situation is that it never becomes impatient, no matter how long it takes the student to "get it." If a teacher worked individually with each student in this way, customizing work to meet each child's special needs and correcting all the papers, he or she could work with only a very few students at a time. "Intelligent" tutoring programs could thus free highly skilled teachers to deal with the more challenging aspects of teaching children with learning disabilities.

Expert systems can also be time-savers. AALPS (Automated Air Load Planning System), for example, advises the U.S. Army's 82nd Airborne Division on how to load cargo into airplanes. The designers of the systems, from California's SRI International (a private research establishment formerly associated with Stanford), interviewed seven experts on loading military cargo. Factors such as load distribution and unevenness of the floors in cargo planes were taken into account, as were key points such as not putting all the ammunition in one plane while the guns travel in another. With AALPS, information on the nature of the cargo and the kinds of planes to be used is fed into the computer, which then advises how to distribute the cargo among the planes. AALPS "knows" how to load 5,000 different types of cargo into five kinds of military planes.

Designing an Expert System

There are two basic components to any expert system—the "knowledge base" and the "rule base." The expert's facts constitute the knowledge base, and the reasoning used to come to decisions reside in the rule base. An expert system can't know more than the experts from whom its knowledge and heuristics came. Designing an expert system is challenging. Knowledge about the domain of the system must be gathered and codified in such a way that it can easily be retrieved. Experts usually do not think about how they evaluate information when deciding a question, so the knowledge engineer must be able to help the expert put into words how he or she goes about solving problems. Everything depends on their successful collaboration. With effort, even "hunches" can sometimes be encoded as rules that an expert system can use.

Altogether, designing an expert system takes a great deal of time, effort, and mental energy. By the time it is completed, it may have been on the drawing board for years and can have 50,000 program lines.

Knowledge and Rules

In some expert systems, the knowledge base is combined with the rules so that any given rule contains the knowledge needed to apply it. Such "production rules" work well for situations where various pieces of information are combined in the rule. Here is an example from MYCIN of a production rule. The rule is stated in LISP code within the system and then translated into English by MYCIN so that the doctor can read it:

IF
1) the infection is primary-bacteremia, and
2) the site of the culture is one of the sterile sites, and
3) the suspected portal of entry of the organism is the gastrointestinal tract,

THEN
there is suggestive evidence (.7) that the identity of the organism is bacteroides.

You don't need to understand the medical jargon to see what MYCIN is doing. Prior to applying this rule, MYCIN will have asked the doctor questions that will tell it if the three conditions of this rule are met. If the answer to one or more of the questions is no, MYCIN will reject this rule and will search to find other rules whose conditions may be met by the data on the patient. One powerful aspect of MYCIN is that it gives an indication of the probability that its conclusions are correct. Note the figure "(.7)" in the THEN statement. This means that there is 70 percent confidence in the conclusion. A figure of 1.0 would indicate complete confidence in the diagnosis.

PROSPECTOR, a program that helps geologists in mineral exploration, clearly separates its knowledge base from the rules. The geologist gives PROSPECTOR observations based on surface features of the area, which are used to determine what sorts of ores could lie underground. PROSPECTOR compares the input to the models in its knowledge base, asks further questions, and eventually comes up with the probabilities that different types of ores may be present.

Kinds of Rules

The rules in an expert system are generally of the IF . . . THEN type, but they can perform different sorts of functions. One kind of rule is absolute—when given data, the rule automatically performs an operation on that data. For example, an expert system managing merchandise for a chain of hardware stores would need a rule for determining the retail cost of the merchandise, based on the wholesale cost. A simple rule can be written to carry out this calculation:

```
RULE: RETAIL PRICE
IF (wholesale price is known)
AND (retail price is unknown)
THEN (calculate retail price
(Retail = Wholesale × 2))
```

With this rule, the expert system would automatically calculate the retail price when given the wholesale price. The new figure would then be added to the knowledge base of the system. (The examples used in this chapter are not stated in exact LISP code but rather in a modified form so that they are easier to understand.)

A "hypothetical rule" might have prevented the 1979 Three Mile Island nuclear plant accident, which led to radioactive contamination of the air. This type of rule tells the expert system to refer to the consequences of situations and to proceed accordingly. If there had been an expert system managing the Three Mile Island plant, it would have noted the stuck valve in the system that caused the trouble. Within its rule base, there would have been a rule roughly like this:

RULE: STUCK VALVE

IF
(or (any valve stuck open)
(any valve stuck closed))
THEN
(notify operator)
(notify repair department)
(hypothesize (valve remains stuck) and explore consequences)

The system would determine if there was any danger in the valve remaining stuck. If it found dangers (and it would have in that case), it would then have notified the operator and the repair department that the valve was stuck and told them the possible consequences of ignoring the stuck valve.

Like other AI programs, expert systems need ways of reducing the number of paths explored. This can be accomplished through the rule base. Rules can be designed to keep a system on the "right track" exploring that path until the end. In the movie *The Wizard of Oz*, Dorothy is told to follow the yellow brick road. Even if it intersected other roads, she always knew which road to follow. An expert system rule to keep Dorothy on the right path would be:

IF (road yellow brick)
THEN (follow this path only)

Rules can take the form of negatives as well—IF this is the case, THEN ignore exploring this path. Most expert systems have both positive and negative rules that help limit the search.

Searching for the Answer

Like other AI programs, expert systems can search in different ways. A system can be "goal driven"—work backward from a possible answer looking for the data, or it can be "data driven"—work from the data toward the solution. MYCIN is a goal-driven system. It picks a hypothetical solution and works backwards through its rules until it finds a rule with an IF statement that needs filling in from the user. Then it asks a question to get the data to complete that statement. Such programs work the way most people do, by forming a hypothesis and then trying to prove it. With this type of system, however, the user can't volunteer information, but must wait until the computer asks before giving data.

PROSPECTOR is a mixed system. The user volunteers the data collected, and the program then searches for possible solutions that the data would satisfy. It may come up with several different possibilities, and ask the user if he or she wants to rule any of them out. If not, the program will explore each, one at a time, asking more questions and evaluating the chosen model based on the data given. At various times, the user can tell PROSPECTOR that a particular path is no longer of interest, and it will be abandoned.

Reviewing Results

The user of an expert system has a lot at stake in accepting the answer. In medical programs, the life of the patient may be at risk. In geological exploration, a great deal of money can be involved. Human users want to know how an expert system makes its way to its conclusions. If the reasoning processes of the system make sense, its conclusions will be more acceptable. Mistakes can be uncovered by asking the computer to explain itself. This capability also eases debugging, as a program could reach the correct conclusion for the wrong reason. Because of this, knowledge engineers like to include a capacity for self-explanation in each expert system.

MYCIN has an auxiliary system called TEIRESIAS that allows humans to communicate directly with MYCIN. Experts can examine the pathway to a diagnosis and can add new information to the system. If an expert finds an error, TEIRESIAS can back up and review the steps it took, until the bug is found. It then aids the expert in fixing the bug by helping put the words into proper form for the computer. TEIRESIAS also enables a user to learn how the experts come to conclusions. In this way, a nonexpert can learn about the thought processes of experts.

How Useful Are They?

The usefulness of an expert system depends on several factors. Most importantly, it must be reasonably accurate. After MYCIN was developed, it was tested by comparing its diagnosis of ten cases with those of eight doctors at Stanford Medical School. Five of the doctors were specialists in the field of infectious diseases, while the other three were younger and less experienced. The therapies suggested by MYCIN and by the doctors were sent to experts who had published medical papers on meningitis diagnosis and treatment. When judged by these experts, MYCIN was given a score of 69 percent correct, which is at first discouraging. But the doctors fared worse—the highest score obtained by any of them was 68 percent. Thus, MYCIN could do better than most doctors, at least in the limited test it was given.

PROSPECTOR has fared better. It uses the expertise of several different specialists and has provided ore-deposit evaluations very close to those of the experts. In addition, PRO-

SPECTOR correctly predicted a molybdenum deposit in the state of Washington that human experts missed—one which may be worth as much as $100 million!

Finally, R1, the system that configures VAX computers, is 99 percent accurate in creating effective designs, a figure surpassing that of human designers.

Speed and ease of use are also important for expert systems, especially when time is a critical factor, as in medicine. MYCIN, despite its reliability, is not often used because it takes too long. By the time a physician finishes answering questions and gets a diagnosis and treatment recommendation from MYCIN, 50 minutes may have gone by. ONCOCIN, which recommends cancer therapy, works differently. It is part of the medical record-keeping system of a hospital. Thus, it always has information about each patient already "digested." When the doctor enters new data, ONCOCIN can recommend treatment right away.

Teaching Machines

Computers have been in use for simple drill work in schools for many years. With AI techniques, however, programs are possible that diagnose the learning difficulties of individual students and design problems especially for each of them. These programs are called Intelligent Tutoring Systems, abbreviated ITS (or ICAA, Intelligent Computer Aided Assistance). ITS are not necessarily expert systems in the strict sense, because their knowledge is not always at the expert level. But the teaching methods they use are often a form of expertise. As with other kinds of artificial intelligence, ITS have run into plenty of problems in development. It is hard enough to get computers to understand grammatical English. But an ITS designed for teaching grammar would have to decipher faulty grammar as well as correct grammer! The same problem would exist for programs designed to tutor foreign language students.

An ITS has to consist of several parts. There must be a knowledge base that "knows" enough about the subject to allow the student to reach the desired level of proficiency. There must be a component that models the different types of difficulties students may have, so that any given student can be classified. A selection of questions, problems, or both, is needed in order to find out what the student knows and what the weak points are. The part of the system that uncovers the student's errors and misconceptions must be able to interact with the question-designing module to individualize the questions, and the material must be presented in accordance with the student's level of understanding.

An attractive feature of some ITS selects questions that relate to the student's personal knowledge. For example, the ITS could ask the student about the sorts of courses he or she has taken. Then, the problems presented could be selected from areas of the student's own knowledge and interest, such as physics or economics.

Mathematics is the easiest area for the development of ITS, since language understanding isn't involved. A good math ITS can pick out consistent errors, inform the student of the correct way of carrying out the operation, and present appropriate problems. For example, the following solutions indicate that the student doesn't understand borrowing and carrying over in subtraction and addition:

$$
\begin{array}{r}
152 \\
- \ 76 \\
\hline
86
\end{array}
\qquad
\begin{array}{r}
243 \\
+ \ 77 \\
\hline
210
\end{array}
$$

While a simple drill program would just keep spitting out addition and subtraction problems to this student, an ITS would present the rules about borrowing and carrying, give examples, and provide sample problems. Instead of practicing the error over and over again, the student would learn the correct way to perform addition and subtraction.

DEBUGGY is an example of a relatively uncomplicated ITS that specializes in subtraction. It can figure out the "bug" in the student's thinking that results in mistakes, make suggestions to the student, and answer the student's questions.

As might be expected, most ITS so far do deal with areas of mathematics, such as math axioms, quadratic equations, and calculus. Other ITS aid in computer programming, tutor geology and meteorology, improve performance on learning games, and analyze medical diagnosis.

One kind of ITS acts as a coach for mastering a computer game. Because children enjoy computer games so much, many educators are interested in their teaching potential. Learning important skills and facts while playing a game can help a child enjoy the learning process and retain the material. One such "computer coach," called WUSOR-II, aids students in playing the game Wumpus. In order to triumph over the computer at Wumpus, the player must know something about geometry, logic, and probability. At the beginning of the game, the player is set down randomly within a maze of caves. The goal is to find the Wumpus and kill it with an arrow. The caves contain various hazards, which produce warnings in adjacent caves, so that the player should be able to avoid them if he or she is thinking logically. If the player makes a bad move, the coach explains why the move is bad and gives the player an opportunity to take it back.

WUSOR-II has four interacting modules. The Expert knows how best to play the game. The Psychologist compares information from the Expert about optimal moves to determine the skill level of the player. This information is passed to the Student Model, which then represents the player's skills as a subset of the Expert's knowledge. Finally, the Tutor uses the Student Model in its interactions with the student. If the student lacks a particular skill that would help him or her make a better move, the Tutor explains that skill.

Prospects for Expert Systems

The possibilities for expert systems are limited only by the imagination of those who might use them and the cooperation of the experts. Experts are busy people, and producing an expert system takes long hours away from other activities, hours that busy people may not want to give up. The idea of having his or her expertise captured by a machine is unsettling to many an expert, while others are reluctant to divulge their secrets to a human knowledge engineer. To get around this last problem, there are now user-friendly programs that allow experts to interact directly with the computer, bypassing the human intermediary.

Medical systems, if organized in a way that allows fast and efficient use, could become a vital part of medical practice. A promising recent medical system is INTERNIST/CADUCEUS, developed by physician Jack Meyers and computer scientist Harry Pople at the University of Pittsburg. INTERNIST/CADUCEUS is a comprehensive expert system that covers over 80 percent of internal medicine. It knows about 500 different diseases and 3,500 possible symptoms. This system will first be used by specialists in internal medicine, but eventually could aid general practitioners, rural health clinics, and physicians' assistants. Good medical expert systems can put the knowledge of top specialists into a form that allows less experienced physicians to give improved treatment and learn at the same time. They can free the specialist to concentrate on the most puzzling and challenging cases. And even after that expert dies, his or her special talent will live on in the expert system and can be updated by additions of new medical knowledge.

With appropriate auxiliary programs, these expert systems could also be used in training new specialists. If, by studying the expert system, young doctors could follow the reasoning used by the best in the field, they could develop their own expertise much more rapidly than with traditional methods of teaching and apprenticing. One such program, called GUIDON, teaches the basic diagnostic principles used in MYCIN. While GUIDON can be helpful, it may have difficulties in fully explaining the problem-solving methods of MYCIN. It turns out that the production-rule approach, while very useful for an ex-

"I THINK WE'LL GET A THIRD OPINION. MY COMPUTER AND I DISAGREE."

Expert systems will become more and more common in future medical practice.
Sidney Harris.

pert system, is not ideal for explaining the reasoning of experts in an educational program. Just how useful GUIDON is, then, will be determined by how useful students find it in practice.

Edward Feigenbaum, geneticist Joshua Lederberg, and chemist Carl Djerassi of Stanford worked together to produce DENDRAL, the first expert system ever, which is now used in laboratories all over the world. DENDRAL sifts through possible chemical structures of organic molecules and chooses those that match the data from particular chemical unknowns. It frees scientists of time-consuming drudgery and can even save laboratories a great deal of money. Because the expertise of many experts is collected in DENDRAL, it makes conclusions based on less detailed data than an individual expert can. According to Feigenbaum, a chemist can determine chemical structures using a $5,000 measuring device with the help of DENDRAL. Without the expert system, the laboratory would need a device with much higher resolution, one that costs around $100,000, in order to reach the same conclusions. As other systems like DENDRAL are produced, more of scientists' time will be available for creative thinking and experimenting, since computers will take over much of the detail work.

New types of expert systems are on the horizon as well. Gregg Collins, a graduate student at Yale University in computer science, has designed an expert system that plays the role of football coach. Collins interviewed Yale coaches to find out how they made their decisions, then put their expertise together. He found that most decisions are based on set rules, that true judgment calls are rare. This made the initial program relatively easy to create. The next step, which is much more difficult, is to get the electronic "coach" to originate its own plays rather than just select plays from a list. To do this, the computer evaluates the reactions of individual players on the opposing team. For each game, unique data would have to be given to the "coach." And when player substitutions were made, the data would have to be changed quickly and correctly.

Expert systems technology holds promise for many programs—ones that manage libraries and help users find information; intelligent tutors for adults; home computer information services that tailor the news to the particular interests of the user; and small-scale programs based on expert-system methods that advise on everything from planting a garden to fixing a clogged sink.

Expert Systems for Business

New developments in small computer hardware are making expert systems and other AI applications more widely available. Personal computers designed to run LISP efficiently, called LISP machines, are now being produced. Businesses that need expert systems and schools that want ITS could become important customers for these computers. As powerful LISP computers become less expensive and users become more acquainted with LISP and its capabilities, expert systems are likely to become commonplace features of modern businesses. Software companies are already selling expert system development software that can help large businesses design their own expert systems.

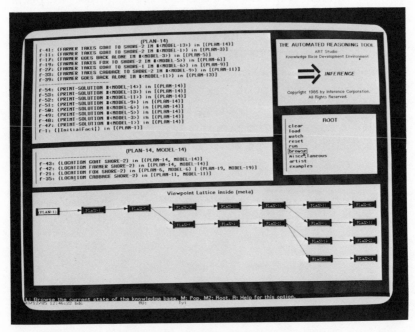

The expert systems development tool called ART indicates its workings in different ways. Displayed on the screen is a solution to the simple problem of a farmer who must take a goat, a cabbage, and a fox across a river one at a time, without leaving the goat and cabbage or the fox and goat together.
Courtesy of Inference Corporation.

For example, Inference Corporation has released ART, a LISP-based programming tool that runs on LISP machines and DEC VAX computers equipped with LISP. Another software package, called EMYCIN (for Essential MYCIN), allows the design of expert systems based on the same principles that underlie MYCIN. EMYCIN also carries with it TEIRESIAS, which helps debug the system, and GUIDON, which adapts it as a teaching tool. Thus, any expert system developed by EMYCIN can explain its reasoning and can be used in instruction as well.

Expert Systems and the Law

Expert systems are generating new social and legal issues. The question of legal responsibility is an especially important problem in medical practice. If a physician consults with INTERNIST/CADUCEUS, for example, and takes its advice, who is responsible for an error in diagnosis? If a patient dies because a particular drug was chosen, or if the recommended treatment leaves a patient with permanent disabilities, can the expert(s) who contributed their knowledge to the system be sued? Is the knowledge engineer, who programmed their expertise, responsible? Or is the attending physician at fault, because he or she chose to consult the system and take its advice?

If persons who suffer because of expert system errors begin suing the experts and the knowledge engineers, the development of new expert systems could well be slowed or halted until these legal questions are settled.

8

AI and Games

AI got off to a promising start with successful game-playing programs. Scientists saw prowess at chess as an ultimate intellectual accomplishment. Newell, Shaw, and Simon (the developers of GPS; see Chapter 1) wrote in 1958: "If one could devise a successful chess machine, one would seem to have penetrated the core of human intellectual endeavor."

Computers that play checkers and backgammon at championship levels now exist, and chess programs now are faster at searching and can therefore consider more positions than ever before. But can true insight into chess ever be programmed into a computer? As with other areas of AI research, the greatest challenge for game programmers is to capture the ability of the top thinkers to use insight rather than merely explore alternatives. Another major problem is the familiar combinatorial explosion. A game program must cut down on the alternatives examined and, in the process, can easily eliminate the best move. A chess Grand Master once remarked, when asked how many moves he considered before choosing: "One—the right one!"

Checkers

In the early days of computers, pioneer Arthur Samuel decided that a program which played checkers could generate interest in computers and perhaps help get funding for the fledgling industry. His interest began in the late 1940's, when he was at the University of Illinois and wanted a computer for the school. He thought that if he and his co-workers could build a small computer and attract public attention, they could get more money for their laboratory. Checkers, they thought, was a trivial game that would be easy to program but would draw lots of public curiosity about their project. Samuel was right about gaining attention, but it wasn't long before he discovered that checkers was far from trivial. Samuel spent approximately the next twenty years developing and improving his checkers program.

Samuel went from Illinois to IBM, where he ran his program on computers as they came off the assembly line, to make sure they had no manufacturing defects. The more experience he had with the program, the more he was able to debug and improve it. The checkers program followed him to Stanford, where he went after retiring from IBM. Samuel's work over the years illustrates some of the important aspects of computer game playing. Even with checkers, a game thought to be relatively simple, there are many more possible moves than the mind can contemplate at once. For each move a player chooses, there are many opposition responses possible. For each of those moves, in turn, the first player would have multiple choices, and so forth. The number of board positions to be examined rapidly becomes unwieldy. Samuel figured that because of the combinatorial explosion, there are about 10^{40} possible moves in a checkers game! Clearly, ways must be found to limit the search of potential moves. Even the fastest computer in the world today would not have time to investigate the ultimate consequences of every possible move.

The alternatives can be narrowed down in a number of ways. One is to incorporate principles used by champion players, thereby developing a game program that is a sort of expert system.

Samuel tried that approach after discovering that general principles of checkers strategy had never been put into print. He consulted with several checkers Masters to find out how they succeeded in winning. But he could never get much out of them, as they found it impossible to verbalize their methods. One of these Masters, who came to Stanford to work with Samuel, became so confused while trying to trace his own thought processes that he quit, fearing that he would mix up his own mind and play worse if he kept trying to analyze his train of thought!

Another way to generate a winning game program is to have it do what humans do—learn from experience. Samuel decided against figuring out how humans learn and then imitating that process; he believed that human learning and machine learning are different because their "hardware" is so different. He designed his program so that positions reached in previous games were stored in memory, along with a number called the "static evaluation function," which indicated the relative advantage to the computer of that move.

Let's look at an example to see how the program worked (see figure following page). The game has reached a board position indicated by A in the diagram, and it is the computer's turn to move. It evaluates the moves it could make next (Column I) by looking at all the opponent's possible moves (Column II) and assuming that, in all cases, the opponent would choose the worst move for the computer. (This technique, in which the computer assumes that the players will always select the best alternative move, is called the "minimax algorithm," or "minimax search.") Then the computer examines its own next move. On the basis of this limited search, the computer picks the move that will result in the best position for itself three moves ahead. Some of the moves it could make (Column III) would give it a higher static evaluation function than the one it chose. However, since it assumes the opponent will play a smart game, the computer must compromise; a move that looks good at first could lead to a disadvantage later.

Once the computer has chosen its moves, it takes the static evaluation function of the expected position at D, which is 8, and stores that number in memory as the "backed-up" value for position A. The backed-up value is more accurate than the static value since it is based on a look-ahead search. The next

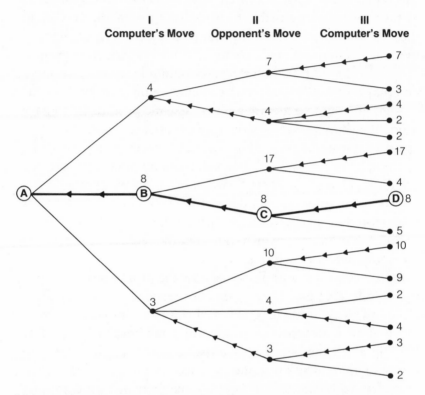

Minimax game tree search in Samuel's checkers program. The computer is in a position indicated (A) in the diagram. In order to choose a move, the computer notes its possible moves (there are 3, column I), then all possible countermoves by its opponent (column II), then its possible responses to those moves (column III). After that, the computer applies a static evaluation function (the numbers next to each of the moves in column III). The higher the value of the function, the better the move is for the computer.

The next step is to "back up" the functions, assuming in each case that both of the players will make the best moves. The highest number from each set of choices in column III is backed up to column II, since it is the computer's turn to move. In column II, it is the opponent's move. The computer assumes the opponent will make its best move, so the *lowest* number from column II must be backed up to column I, since it represents the opponent making the move in its best interest. It is again the computer's move in column I, and the highest number from column I, which is 8, is backed up to position (A). The computer then stores that number as the "backed-up value" for position (A).

time the computer is in a game where position A is a possibility, it need not recalculate the function, since it is already stored in memory. Thus, as the program plays more games, its search becomes easier and quicker.

By storing the backed-up values, Samuel's program could improve the depth of its searches the more games it played. For example, if the computer reached position E (see figure below) in a later game and was searching three moves ahead as usual, it would recognize that it had experienced position A in a previous game and, by using the backed-up value of A, would have the advantage of looking three further moves ahead for position A, without having to make any more calculations. Eventually, instead of just looking three moves ahead, the program could sometimes see all the way to the end of the game when it encountered moves it had previously made.

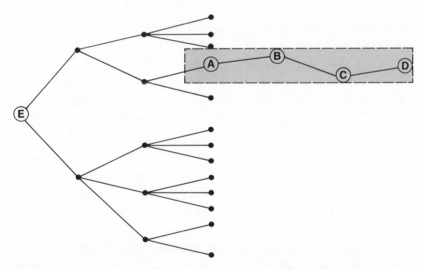

How rote learning helps future play in Samuel's checkers program. In a later game, the computer is at position (E). As before, it looks ahead three moves. One of the possible positions at the third move is the same encountered in the previous figure. The computer has a back-up value of 8 associated with position (A) in its memory, which is a much better estimate of how good that move is than the static evaluation functions it must apply to the other positions. The more the computer plays, the more positions will have backed-up values associated with them, and the more accurately it will be able to estimate the effectiveness of its moves.

Samuel's program was trained by playing against itself, playing through published games of accomplished players, and playing against humans, including Masters. By 1959, the program had become a better-than-average novice. The only learning method used by the program up to this point was pure rote memory. At the beginning of a game, the computer could play quite well, as there are a limited number of moves early on. In the middle of the game, when many moves are possible, rote learning was much less effective in improving play.

Toward the game's end, when winning and losing positions could be recognized, the program ran into a curious difficulty. When the computer was in a good position near the end, the values associated with all moves tended to be high and identical or nearly so. Almost any move could eventually result in a win, and the computer wandered aimlessly about the board, unable to end the game quickly. Samuel solved this problem by adding more information to the program. He included, with each board position and its value, another number indicating the length of the path to the game's end, and he changed the move selector to pick the position with the highest value *and* the shortest path. This way, the program would move along toward the earliest victory or, if it was losing, would "stall" as long as possible.

This early version of Samuel's checkers program taught researchers a great deal about AI techniques. They saw that rote learning was a powerful tool, but that it could allow a program to progress only to a certain point in proficiency. During the 1960's, Samuel added more sophisticated learning techniques to his program, which improved its performance a great deal. It reached the masters' level of play and was able to defeat some top players. However, the very best still beat it. In 1965, the world champion, W. F. Hellman, won all four games he played against the computer. Even with checkers, reaching the highest level of competence is difficult for a computer program.

Chess

Chess is far, far more complex than checkers. Since 1957, many AI researchers have designed programs for playing this game, using a variety of techniques in an attempt to achieve world class status. Every year since 1970, a North American Computer Chess Champion has been chosen at a tournament sponsored by the Association for Computing Machinery. There is also a World Computer Chess Championship contest. Computer chess programs have gotten good enough that the United States Chess Federation has given high ratings to at least 25 of them.

Chess players are rated at levels starting from Class E and moving to Class A, then Expert, Master, and Senior Master. In international competition, there are the additional rankings of International Master and International Grand Master. The 1984 American and World Computer Chess Champion, the Cray Blitz, ranks as a "high expert."

The effects of the combinatorial explosion in chess can be overwhelming. Claude Shannon, an AI pioneer interested in chess, calculated that 10^{120} plays are possible in an average chess game. For a chess player to be successful, he or she must be able to look ahead several moves to see the possible consequences of a play. But if a computer is programmed to look ahead six moves from its position—three for itself and three for its opponent—it would have to examine about a billion possible plays at the sixth move. World champion players are known to look ahead as far as 20 moves, and an Expert player is likely to need to explore 14 or more moves ahead at least once in a game. Obviously, the great human players are able to manage the problem. But how can a chess computer be put together to accomplish this task?

The first computer chess program to achieve Expert status against humans, Chess 4.5, dealt with the combinatorial explosion by compromising. It explored all reasonable legal moves to a depth of 2 (2 moves ahead) and chose a move on that basis. Then, it searched to a depth of 3 and then 4, and so forth, until reaching a time limit. As with Samuel's checkers program, results of searches were saved for later use. In tournament play, Chess 4.5 explored to an average of 500,000 nodes on the search tree, usually to 6 moves ahead on each turn. This exhaustive search was possible because it ran on a very fast computer.

Belle is a specialized chess machine. It was created by two Bell Labs scientists, Ken Thompson, right foreground, and Joe Condon, left, both affiliated with the Computing Science Research Center.
Courtesy of AT&T Bell Laboratories.

Another fast program, Belle, designed at Bell Laboratories, can examine 130,000 positions a second.

The Cray Blitz

Chess programs employ many strategies, but the ability to carry out an extensive search is still an important key to success for machine chess. The Cray Blitz runs on a Cray XMP-48 super-computer, one of the fastest machines around. The XMP has four processors instead of one, so it can follow four different

Playing chess against a computer can be a strange experience for a person.
Courtesy of Chess Life.

paths at one time. Using the XMP is the equivalent of having four computers working at once.

The Cray Blitz program was begun in 1976 by Bob Hyatt, with the help of Albert Gower, both from the University of Southern Mississippi. They have been aided by Harry Nelson of the Lawrence Livermore National Laboratory. These patient men have devoted an estimated 32,000 hours to the program, painstakingly entering about 100,000 early game positions and their evaluations. The Cray Blitz program does not always follow the classic "book" moves. Hyatt and Gower didn't agree with all the information in chess books, so they designed their program to make unconventional plays now and then. It is also programmed to choose its own play when the best one isn't clear. This results sometimes in some truly peculiar moves.

When a human knows something about a computer's strategy, he or she can use it to defeat the machine. David Levy of Intelligent Software Ltd. in London, England, is an International Grand Master as well as a computer scientist. Levy has a long-standing challenge against chess computers and has offered a financial reward to the designers of a program that can beat him. In 1984, Levy defeated the Cray Blitz 4–0 in a contest over the international telephone wires. His strategy was to use plays that humans might deem inferior but that the computer would have trouble "understanding." The Cray Blitz is still far from meeting human standards of chess greatness. It may soon achieve Master rating, but this is well below International Master and far from International Grand Master.

Hitech

The 1985 North American Computer Chess Champion, Hitech, is the creation of former World Correspondence Chess Champion Hans Berliner, Carl Eberling, and a group of coworkers at Carnegie-Mellon University. Hitech uses a new architecture and new searching methods to get around the combinatorial explosion. Hitech has 64 specially designed chips, each of which represents a square on the chess board. When Hitech looks at possible moves, the positions of the pieces on the chess board are communicated to these chips, and each chip generates all possible legal moves to its square on the board and produces a value for the best move. A central decision unit then chooses the best-appearing move from among the chips to be tried first. Later, the second-best-appearing move may have to be investigated, if the previous choice did not work out.

Hitech can examine 175,000 moves a second; it is 50 percent faster at generating moves than any other machine to date. But the real secret of its success lies in its parallel structure and in how its knowledge is organized. Each of the 64 chips operates independently of the others so that there is no bottleneck in generating the next move to be tried. After only a few months of playing, Hitech reached Master ranking, and its creators plan to refine and expand its chess knowledge. They will probably increase the evaluation units from 8 to 32. Because of the way the system is organized, this significant expansion of the knowledge base will not slow down the searching process significantly. With Hitech, computer chess may finally have reached the point where it will be a real challenge to the best human players.

Backgammon

The one computer game program that has beaten the world champion is BKG 9.8, Hans Berliner's famous backgammon program. In July 1979, BKG 9.8 defeated Luigi Villa 7 to 1, winning $5,000 for its creator. Berliner tried many techniques in designing his program before finally settling on the best method, which emphasizes analyzing the relative value of different board positions instead of searching through hundreds of alternative moves as chess programs do. During the competition, BKG played very well, but moves in backgammon are determined by throwing dice, so an element of luck enters into the game. After the big match, Berliner carefully analyzed the entire competition and decided that, although his program played well, its human opponent had actually played better and had made fewer mistakes, while the computer had gotten better throws of the dice.

9

Computer Perception— Vision and Speech Recognition

As you read this page, your eyes quickly recognize the words, and your brain almost instantly gives them meaning. When someone enters the room, you look up and immediately recognize the human form and identify who it is. And when that person speaks to you, you have no trouble at all understanding the words. Seeing and hearing come so easily to us that perception, like natural language understanding, was first not recognized as a challenging issue. Legend has it that a pioneering AI researcher once gave a graduate student a small, manageable summer project—"solve vision"! That was twenty years ago, and despite years of intense research, we are still a long way from effective computer vision. Industrial robots can recognize the outline of the part they are to manipulate, but that's about all. Voice recognition has progressed further; primitive systems are available even for personal computers. Computers that can understand the natural language of a variety of users, however, are still in the future.

Problems with Perception

Hearing and sight share certain features that make them difficult for computers to interpret. Both are sensed as responses of nerve cells to stimuli from the environment. Sound waves reaching the ear stimulate the eardrum to vibrate. The vibrations are picked up by tiny bones in the middle ear, which passes them on to fluid in the inner ear, where sensory cells fire in response to the movements of the fluid. The electrical signals from the ear are then passed to the brain by way of the auditory nerve. The eye works in a similar fashion, although the system is more complex (see below). The brain must somehow make sense of the stream of electrical signals from these sense organs.

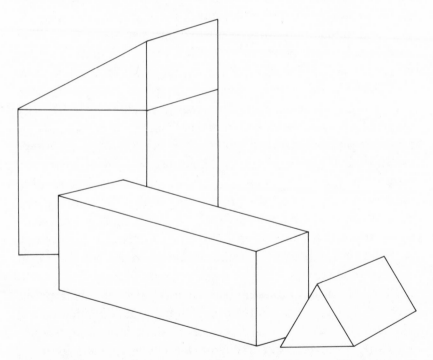

An arrangement of blocks in which some blocks partially obscure the view we have of others. We can easily figure out the correct shapes of the blocks, but it is difficult to get a computer to do so.

When we see and hear, the stimulation of our senses is usually continuous. Our eyes see a whole scene, and our brains effortlessly separate that scene into individual, understandable objects. Our ears take in a continuous stream of sound when another person speaks. Our brains know where one word ends and another begins and automatically assign appropriate meanings to those words. How does the brain accomplish these tasks so easily? And how can we get computers to simulate these feats?

Approaching the Problem

When researchers attempt to mechanize sensory understanding, they must divide the processes into stages that are at least analogous to those undertaken by our sensory systems. First of all, the continuous input must be divided into separate pieces. With speech, the sound waves are recorded and the amplitude of the waves is measured at fixed intervals, for example, 20,000 times a second. The first step in vision is a "map" of the light intensity at each point in the image. White areas have a high light intensity while black areas have low intensity. Such a map is made by taking a picture with a digital camera that divides the image into a grid of individual points. Each point is called a "pixel," an abbreviation for "picture element." Each pixel is given a numerical value, depending on its brightness. The more pixels per unit of area, the finer the detail captured. Thus a black-and-white scene, when analyzed by a visual system, is represented by rows and columns of numbers, one number for each dot. Each number represents a particular shade of gray.

After the sensory input has been divided into individual pieces, they are grouped into appropriate units—sounds (such as are phonetically indicated in a dictionary to show how to pronounce a word) for speech, and recognizable elements, such as lines, for vision. Then the units must be identified and labeled in some way—they must be assigned a value, such as the sound "s" or the label "edge of a figure." There is a problem here, for often in vision it is not possible at this stage to determine the value of a unit. A line might be the edge of an object or it might be part of a pattern, such as stripes on a zebra. In order to determine the correct label for a visual unit, a list of alternatives may be assigned to it and the correct interpretation made at a later stage, when more information is available. Or, the entire image may be examined to provide more clues. A pattern of like units, for example, might indicate the label "edge of stripe," whereas no pattern might mean "edge of an object."

After all the units are labeled, they must be reassembled into meaningful elements such as individual words or objects in a scene. This is the hardest part of the process, for so much depends on that troublesome concept we have met before, context. For speech, context involves a variety of factors, such as age and sex of speaker, mood, and type of communication. Vision involves even more contextual elements—direction and number of light sources (which will determine shadows), degree of movement, complexity of the scene being viewed, the type of situation involved, and so forth.

More About Vision

Studies of vision, like those of natural language and common sense, inspire awe for the complexity and accuracy of the human brain. At the back of the human eye is the retina, a disk-shaped area of light-sensitive cells that fire signals to other neurons when struck by light. There are at least ten million of these cells, and they overlie four other layers of neurons, through which they communicate information to the optic nerve, which leads to the brain. Within the retina of one eye, about 10 billion calculations are made each second. Thus, before information about the perceived image reaches the optic nerve, it has already been processed and altered in unknown ways. Even the fastest modern computers can't handle all this information. It would take a Cray supercomputer a hundred years or more to duplicate the neural events that take place several times a second in one eye!

Once the message from the retina reaches the brain, it is

further processed in more than a dozen different regions within the cerebral cortex. Analyzing visual images is so complex, as a matter of fact, that it uses about sixty percent of the neurons in the cerebral cortex.

We take for granted our ability to recognize and interpret what we see. But if you think about it, you can begin to realize how elaborate the visual process is. Every visual cell on the retina reacts to a minute point of light coming from the environment. That light has a certain intensity and color. The visual system and the brain must be able to take the millions of tiny bits of information about visual input coming continuously from both eyes and integrate them into a single, understandable, three-dimensional image. The brain does much more than create a picture like that produced by a camera; it also interprets the image and understands what it represents. And unlike a still

We know at a glance what each of these six simple drawings represents. How does the brain extract the essential elements of an image and identify it?

photo, what we see is almost constantly in motion, adding yet another intricate dimension to interpret.

What Does It Mean?

Interpreting visual input is very similar to applying "common sense" in understanding natural language. We recognize particular objects as belonging to certain classes without thinking about it. A tree, for example, will be recognized whether it is a tall, slim, dark green pine; a broadly outstretched maple with flaming red leaves; a stark, bare elm in the middle of winter; or a green-crowned palm on a desert island. If most of the tree is hidden by a house, we still know it is a tree, and we can even imagine the shape of the part that is hidden.

We can recognize two-dimensional, man-made trees in paintings and cartoons as being trees, too, even when they possess only the basics of "treeness." Thus, our brains must contain some sort of stored image of the essence of objects we will encounter in the environment, and they can identify these objects from any number of views, in any color or size, and in a great variety of forms. Without thinking, we classify the objects our eyes see and combine them into coherent images that we understand and react to in an instant.

Vision is so important to human understanding of the world that visual input overrides that from all our other senses. You have probably had the experience of sitting in a car in a parking lot and daydreaming, only to react with surprise when the next car begins to back up. For a moment, you think that you are traveling forward, despite the fact that your body senses no movement. This effect shows the dominance of vision. Watching a movie that depicts a roller coaster ride has an even more striking result. Scientists have studied this phenomenon by placing a person in a room and projecting the image of a slowly rotating drum onto the wall. The person attempts to walk normally but keeps stumbling as if trying to maintain balance on the rotating floor of the drum. Optical illusions, too, are an indication that we "believe" our eyes even if they deceive us.

From Image to Understanding

The nervous system uses algorithms of some sort to solve the problems of visual interpretation. These algorithms can sometimes lead to false conclusions, but generally they lead to useful interpretations. If scientists can unravel how the visual system goes about interpreting input, they can work on ways of programming computers to do the same.

At MIT's Artificial Intelligence Laboratory, researchers use solid-state electronic sensors to measure the light intensity of images. The result is an array of 1,000 by 1,000 pixels for each scene. The image projected on the human retina has far more individual elements, so the experimental image is not as sharp as the natural one. But the same principles can be applied to it, once we know what those principles are.

Your eyes provide many clues for interpreting what you see. For example, when you look at a point in the visual field, each eye sees it from a slightly different angle. If you alternately close each of your eyes, the image that you see shifts slightly in position. The visual system uses the clues from the two eyes to determine distance and to aid in establishing the shapes of objects. At MIT, some researchers are concentrating on how this stereoscopic vision—called "stereopsis"—works. The late Dr. David Marr was a pioneer in this area, and other scientists, such as Dr. Tomaso Poggio, are continuing to unravel the mysteries of stereopsis. One question MIT scientists are exploring is how the visual system "knows" which point on one retina corresponds to a particular point on the other retina. Just how the nervous system goes about fitting together the images from the two eyes into a three-dimensional representation turns out to be a very complicated problem. Marr and Poggio developed one algorithm that works fairly well when used on a computer and may also be used by our visual system. It is able to accomplish limited analysis of aerial photographs and shows some characteristics of depth perception.

Computers are still a long way from imitating the visual abilities of humans. Just inventing industrial robots that can recognize and manipulate single parts in assembly line production is a demanding venture. Current robots can pick up a part only when it is oriented in a specific way on the conveyor belt. But robots that can recognize the part when it is mixed in a pile and then "figure out" how to pick it up are a real challenge to design.

Researchers are intensively probing other aspects of vision, too. Vision research was long underway in psychology and physiology laboratories before computer scientists became interested in the problem, and findings in one type of study often stimulate new research ideas in others. AI vision research is complementary to that of psychologists and neurophysiologists. AI scientists work largely on the processes that occur between the impact of light on the retinal cells (the concern of the neurophysiologists) and the ultimate interpretation by the brain of what is seen (the realm of the psychologist). Their investigations indicate several levels at which the visual input is processed before being interpreted by the brain. Many "clues" from the input are used to "understand" what we see. In addition to studying stereopsis, AI researchers are working on how information is extracted from movement, how the shape of objects can be determined from their shading, how the visual system separates continuous input into separate shapes or objects, and other aspects of how the visual system works. Because many kinds of interpretation of visual images almost certainly occur simultaneously in the nervous system, a linear von Neuman machine (see Chapter 2) with a single microprocessor that handles data sequentially cannot deal with the complexity of visual understanding. Ultimately, truly effective visual interpretation systems will probably not come into being until computers with many microprocessors working in parallel have been perfected (see Chapter 13).

Speech Recognition

Take all the problems of natural language understanding and multiply them by an unknown but large number, and you have some idea how hard it is to get computers to understand human speech. The obstacles are awesome. But the payoff could be handsome. A computer system that could understand continuous natural speech as it is being uttered would have almost endless uses. A spacecraft commander with both hands at the controls could give his vehicle additional vital instructions with his voice. A busy executive could have important correspondence printed as it was dictated or have data fed directly into a computer when spoken. Writers who think best aloud would be freed from the burden of having to type their creations on a typewriter or computer. The list goes on and on.   .

There are two approaches to speech recognition—"front end" and "back end." Front end approaches deal with how the computer recognizes the sounds it "hears." The phonetics of the input and the way the signals are processed are examples of front end problems. Back end methods are concerned with aspects more closely allied to AI research—sorting out ambiguities by looking at the context and the structure of the language.

In the United States, Fred Jelinek of IBM is working on a voice-activated typewriter (VAT) that can recognize 5,000 words and can keep up with a person speaking at normal speed. Ray Kurzweil, who has already invented a reading machine for the blind and a versatile music synthesizer, is developing a VAT that will have a 10,000 word vocabulary. Speakers will have to make brief pauses between words to use his machine. Both the IBM and Kurzweil VATs will require "training time" with users so that they can recognize the users' particular speech patterns. The Japanese are also working hard on this problem, as part of their Fifth Generation project (see Chapter 13). Their goal is to produce an automatic typewriter with a 50,000 word vocabulary that can understand the continuous speech of many different speakers.

Overcoming Ambiguity

The ambiguities of spoken language are even more striking than those of the written word. A very basic problem is getting a computer to find the divisions between words in phrases such as "gas station" or "time machine." Perhaps in these cases, the computer could scan its memory and find only one way of separating the syllables into two English words. But what if there is more than one way to interpret the syllables? The word pairs "cat scares" and "cat's cares" sound almost the same. "The cat's cares are few" and "The cat scares the birds away" use those syllables in very different ways. The other words in the sentence allow the human mind to understand the difference, but programming this sort of feedback into a computer isn't easy. Not only that, but "the cat scares are few" could be the correct interpretation of the syllables, rather than "the cat's cares are few," if the discussion concerns the well-being of the neighborhood bird population. Here, the context of the sentence would make the meaning clear to us, but would involve more complex programming of the computer. Even entire sentences can sound the same to a machine. A favorite example is the following pair of sentences—"It's hard to wreck a nice beach" and "It's hard to recognize speech." These two sentences may sound different to people, but to a machine, they are virtually identical.

When we speak, we don't always pronounce a particular word the same way. The emphasis and tone of the word vary, depending on its position in the sentence and the meaning we want to convey. Much of this is an unconscious part of our speech patterns, but sometimes we do it on purpose. The word "the," for example, is pronounced one way most of the time but a different way when we want to emphasize the uniqueness of an individual object.

One of the greatest challenges for speech understanding is figuring out how to get a computer to unravel regional accents. If you have ever conversed with a person from a part of the country where the accent is very different, you might have some sympathy for the computer! In Boston, the letter "r" is often ignored, as in the oft quoted phrase, "Pahk yuh cah in Hahvuhd Yahd" ("Park your car in Harvard Yard"). Even the subtle variations in pronouniation in areas where "standard" American speech is used could throw a machine. In parts of the Midwest, "wash" comes out "warsh," while in the Mountain Northwest, a "wolf" is a "woof," and a "roof" rhymes with it.

And finally, even in a particular region of the country, individuals have their own speech patterns and their own vocal ranges. Women tend to have high voices and men low ones. Some people talk fast while others speak slowly. Some pronounce clearly and others slur their words together. Until flexible programs can be developed that can deal with all these differences, true speech recognition will be only a dream.

Understanding Music

Another way to approach the understanding of sound signals is to work with music. Efforts at getting computers to interpret music are underway in several AI laboratories. At Stanford University, a program has been developed that can listen to a single line of music and put it down on paper in musical notation. While this process is very simple for a musically trained human, it is tough for a computer. First, the music must be broken down acoustically. In the Stanford program, the computer samples the sound 30,000 times a second, resulting in samples 16 bits wide. The pitches are identified and their timing is calculated. Then, the music must be further taken apart to figure out the tempo, key, and note values of the piece. Heuristic methods are necessary in analyzing the music, for there are often several possible choices of how the music should be interpreted. For example, when a beat is divided up so that two identical notes are played, the computer must decide whether the two notes are of equal value or if one is longer than the other. The human ear can hear and understand these differences quite well, but sometimes the computer has to guess.

Some musical styles are easier for the computer than others. Composers such as Mozart, who wrote with a degree of mathematical precision, are simplest to decipher. The Stanford program was thrown for a loop when first given Scott Joplin's ragtime piano music to analyze. After being provided with information about the syncopated rhythms that characterize ragtime, the computer could handle it. Contemporary serious music is very difficult for the Stanford machine because it rarely follows recognizable patterns, making heuristic analysis almost impossible.

10

Robots

Man, in his desire for a life of ease and luxury, had created the robots. In his conceit, he had constructed most of them in his own likeness, or at least with some resemblance to that which he considered as the ideal of physical being. . . . This was particularly so of the robot-surgeon. The marvelous mechanisms were housed in a body like a Greek god's, the covering of which was made from an elastic, tinted material that had all the feel and appearance of human flesh and epidermis. The electric-eye lenses looked like human optics and moved in their sockets in a most lifelike manner. There was a wig of curly brown hair, as well as eyelashes and brows. . . . He was man's most perfect servant. Every verbal instruction he carried out to the letter. . . . His memory never failed . . . [his] mechanical brain recorded everything. Without further attention, he would labor twenty-four hours a day. . . . No supervising human mind was needed.

This ideal servant of humankind was described in the story "Rex," written in 1934 by Harl Vincent. Rex had the honor of being the first electronically operated robot in science fiction, but the idea of machines that look and function like people has captured the human imagination for generations. In the nineteenth century, Herman Melville ("The Bell Tower"), Samuel Butler ("The Book of Machines"), and Ambrose Bierce ("Moxon's Master") wrote intelligent machines into their stories. The term "robot" was coined by the Czech writer Karel Capek in

1921, for his play, *R.U.R.* (*Rossum's Universal Robots*). The word is derived from the Czech word for work, or required service, "robota."

The concept of robots as mechanical imitations of humans fascinates people, but it is questionable just how humanlike robots can be.
Sidney Harris.

While people are fascinated by the idea of robots, we have also been concerned about their potential power—if we create them, can we control them? In 1942, the science and science fiction writer Isaac Asimov put forth his famous Three Laws of Robotics in the story "Runaround." Ever since, the Three Laws have been quoted and referred to in countless stories and articles about robots, for they provide a solution to the problem of robot "morality." Asimov's laws are:

> 1) A robot may not injure a human being, nor through inaction allow a human being to come to harm.
> 2) A robot must obey the orders given it by human beings except where such orders would conflict with the First Law.
> 3) A robot must protect its own existence as long as such protection does not conflict with the First or Second Law.

The popular concept of robots is of machines that can walk, use their arms, hear, and speak, like C-3PO in the *Star Wars* films. C-3PO's companion, R2-D2, is also a robot, even though it rolls around on wheels rather than walking and doesn't speak a human language. The reality of robots, however, is a great deal less advanced. Many machines of different kinds are used in factories, and some have been around for a long time. Just which ones are called "robots" may be a matter of choice, since they range from purely mechanical gadgets to highly programmable "robots" that can be adapted to different sorts of work. Perhaps the best way to define robots is to say that robots are machines controlled by way of computer hardware and software.

Robots are very valuable in industry. They perform repetitive tasks without getting bored or tired, and they can work in unpleasant or dangerous places without complaint. Mobile robots can work in environments that are very dangerous for humans—deep within nuclear power plants, for instance, or on the surface of faraway planets. Because robots show such promise, their development is a very active part of AI.

Why AI?

You might wonder why robotics is classified as a part of AI research. Robots present the same problems of flexibility, uncertainty, and knowledge access that arise in programming for natural language understanding, common sense, and perception. For example, when a robot must move about on its own over varied terrain, it encounters difficulties associated with responding to real-world situations. Heuristic rules must be used in making decisions about how robots move. When an animal places its foot on the ground, it doesn't always know ahead of time what is in store. Its foot could land on a hard, uneven rock or on a soft spot of ground. The ground could be easy to grip or slippery. The ground level could be higher or lower than where the foot previously landed. All these uncertainties mean that robot movement must be programmed flexibly. The robot must use heuristic methods to "decide" where to put down its feet and how hard to press. It must have alternative plans in case it comes up against an obstacle. Furthermore, it needs ways to recognize when it has completed a programmed task so it can go on to the next one. All these requirements put robotics squarely into the AI arena, even when the research involved includes only the problem of locomotion.

Robots in Industry

Industrial robots are already taking on significant roles in certain kinds of manufacturing. Japan uses more robots than any other industrial nation. In 1982, there were 77,000 robots at work in Japan, which constituted almost 70 percent of all the robots in the world. Robots are at the heart of Japanese auto industry success. Using robots, a Japanese automobile manufacturer can produce 30 to 40 cars a day per human worker, up from five or six a day before robots.

Since the problems associated with performance in unpre-. dictable environments have yet to be solved, current working robots are able to carry out only limited jobs. They are not the walking, talking robots of science fiction; they are stationary, and their moving parts usually consist merely of an arm that performs a task. These robots must be "trained" by an experienced human worker to do the necessary work. The person moves the robot arm through the appropriate motions, which are recorded on a memory device so that the robot can repeat them without human aid. From then on, the robot plays back the instructions for movement over and over again and performs the assigned task repeatedly. These playback robots are very useful in many repetitive jobs—for example, spot welding, painting, and loading.

Early Experimental Robots

During the 1960's, big robotics projects were conducted at MIT, Stanford University, Edinburgh University in Scotland, and SRI International. Three of these projects—at MIT, Stanford, and Edinburgh—involved only eye-hand coordination. There was a television camera "eye" connected to a computer "brain" that interpreted the visual input from the eye and coordinated it with the movements of a mechanical arm or arms that had a grasping hand or hands. These robots worked in a "blocks world" environment similar to that later simulated in Terry Winograd's SHRDLU project (see Chapter 6). The Stanford robot arm graduated from the blocks world to a real world problem. It could successfully put together an automobile water pump from parts scattered randomly on a tabletop.

Coordinating an electronic eye with a mechanical arm by means of a computer to find the parts, pick them up, and assemble them in the correct order was a major accomplishment. When you pick something up, several senses are involved. First, you see the object and note its position. Then, you move your hand toward it while sensors within your arm keep your body aware of your arm's position. When your hand touches the item, your eyes see it happen, and touch receptors in your hand feel the surface of the object. As your fingers grasp it, pressure receptors sense its hardness and feel how tightly your fingers are closing, allowing your hand to stop pressing when it has a good hold without crushing the object.

While the three stationary robots were rather boring to watch, the fourth model was a popular success. The SRI robot looked rather like a crude robot from the human imagination. Given the name "Shakey," because of the uneven way it traveled, the SRI robot was visited by schoolchildren and scientists alike. Shakey could move around the floor on its wheels and would turn when it bumped into an obstacle. It had a television camera that allowed some vision and a radio antenna that connected it to its controlling computer.

By the mid-1970's, even though these four projects had produced some results, funding for robot projects dried up. Only in the early 1980's, with progress in vision research, more powerful chips that allowed robots to carry more of their "brains" around with them, and new funding from the government for the development of military robots (see Chapter 13), did robot research pick up again.

Ways of Walking

As humans, we are used to two-legged walking, and we imagine robots getting about on two legs as we do. However, balance is not easy on two legs. Mobile robots that will function indoors commonly have wheels, so they can roll easily from place to place without having to deal with balance. But wheels, like two legs, have their limitations over rough ground. Even four-wheel-drive vehicles cannot always make it over soft or very uneven terrain, and if you have ever accompanied a dog on a romp in the woods, you can appreciate the advantages of having more than two legs for efficient locomotion. The most flourishing group of land animals on earth, the insects, owe much of their success to their six-leggedness. Six legs are enough to keep a creature in balance, but not so many that it loses agility. Because of the advantage of six legs, the first American walking machines have used this design.

This is Shakey, the first mobile robot, which was developed at SRI International in Menlo Park, California.
Courtesy of SRI International.

Insects generally move by keeping three legs on the ground—say the left first and third and right middle legs—while lifting up the other three and moving them forward. Then these three are set down and the other trio is lifted. In this way, the animal always has a firm tripod supporting its body, so the problems of balance are minimized. Six-legged walking machines use the same principle, keeping at least three legs on the ground at a time.

In order to navigate over rough ground, the machine must be able to figure out where and how to place its legs. It must have sensors that can determine the horizontal angle of the leg and the amount of weight it carries. The leg should have an adjustable length and/or bendable joints that can adjust to high and low spots. These are just a few of the factors that robot leg designers must take into account.

Other Considerations

Robots represent perhaps the greatest challenge of AI, especially if the goal is to produce a walking, talking machine that can find its way about and follow commands given in natural language. We have already seen how difficult these problems are. With robots they are made even more complex, for the functions of a robot must be integrated with one another. The visual system must not only analyze images, it must also be able to figure out the significance of what it "sees" and communicate that to the moving parts. The natural language system must not only respond to the human operator, it must also relay the instructions on what to do next to the sensory and motor components of the robot. Integrating all the parts in a reliable fashion is, to say the least, a gigantic task.

A robot that moves around and functions in the real world will regularly encounter surprises, for the world is unpredictable. For example, the robot will encounter obstacles and will have to search about for objects. If it keeps making the same blunders and getting stymied, a robot would not be very useful. A robot that cannot detect errors and correct them—that is, learn from its mistakes—would be very limited. In addition to avoiding repeated errors, a robot must be able to generate its own plans for getting out of trouble, which is yet another very tough programming job.

Robot Futures

Despite all the problems posed by robot development, people are enthusiastic about the possible applications. Robots could, for example, be very useful in hospitals. Larry Leifer, a professor of mechanical engineering at Stanford, is working with researchers at the Palo Alto Veterans Administration Medical Center to develop robot aids for disabled patients. They are using a two-fingered robot arm with optical sensors that can judge the distance to objects by bouncing light off them and measuring the intensity of the rays that return. The arm can be extended 18 inches and can move up, down, left, right, forward, and back, on voice command. It can recognize 58 words and can also be controlled by a joystick to carry out a specific sequence of commands. As robots become more and more sophisticated, Leifer plans to adapt the newer versions to helping the disabled. In addition to "life-size" robots, tiny robots could be used for medical diagnosis, with minute television cameras inserted into the body to find and perhaps even repair internal damage without surgery.

Sentry robots that guard airfields, prisons, and large businesses already exist. The model made by Denning Mobile Robotics, Inc., weights 300 pounds and has an advanced navigation system that allows it to patrol prisons and warehouses. It can also wash floors in large buildings such as supermarkets and airports. The Prowler, from Robot Defense Systems, is a mobile sentry that looks like a tank and can be armed with guns. The Prowler has an optional feature requiring a human okay before opening fire. The company doesn't think that The Prowler will be equipped with lethal weapons when used in the United States, but some foreign buyers are interested in armed versions.

Robots are being developed in the United States for quality control in automated factories. For example, a television eye that evaluates the fat content of bacon is being manufactured by the Arthur D. Little Company. Donald L. Sullivan, its developer, says that the eye produces a grid of 76,000 pixels that represents a slice of bacon. Each pixel is evaluated, with very dark ones assigned as background, light ones as fat, and medium ones as strips of meat in the bacon. The robot can then accept or reject the bacon slice, based on its fat content. Robots of this type can also be used to check for burned crackers, broken seals on boil-in bags of frozen food, and so on.

Household Robots

The ultimate robot, of course, is the humanlike machine that can carry out just about any command reliably and without complaint. Because of the attractiveness of this robot image, household robots are already taking hold of the popular imagination, even though they are not able to accomplish much yet. Experts predict that a useful, reliable household robot may come about by the 1990's but will be quite expensive.

Meanwhile, consumers are showing great interest in the simple personal robots now available. Hero 1, from the Heath Corporation, can be bought assembled or in a kit. Hero can accept programs that have been written on other computers and transferred into its memory. It can be directly programmed, too. Hero has a head that turns and an arm that can lift up to one pound. It can "talk" through its own voice synthesizer and can be controlled with a joystick connected by a cable. Like an industrial robot, Hero can be programmed by having the user take it through a series of movements and push a button to lock them into memory. Hero 1 has a "little brother," called Hero Jr., that will wander about randomly when not told what to do. Upon bumping into a wall, Hero Jr. will mutter, "Who put that here?" B.O.B. (Brain On-Board), made by Androbot in Sunnyvale, California, is another American model. B.O.B. looks rather like a Hollywood robot, with a headlike top that has eyes and a smiling "mouth." B.O.B. cannot pick up or manipulate objects itself, but it can pull along an "Androwagon" loaded with objects. B.O.B. can be programmed to patrol the house and shout "Burglar! Burglar!" with its voice synthesizer. It even has an optional onboard refrigerator for serving drinks! The Omnibot, from Japan, can also follow a route you "teach" it. The memory stores up to seven programs that can be performed automatically at any time the owner wishes. Omnibot 2000 has an adept robot arm that can pick up a bottle and pour drinks without spilling a drop.

Because of their special appeal, personal robots may flood the market soon, as did personal computers a few years ago. We are likely to see a great variety of features in these new machines. However, it will be several years before they exhibit much in the way of true artificial intelligence.

11

AI and
Personal Computers

What is the meaning of artificial intelligence research for home and office computer users? Can AI techniques provide helpful programs for personal computers? Already, the phrase "artificial intelligence" is used in advertising some software products. But true AI requires more memory than most personal computers now possess. A simple AI application may need 1,024K bytes (one megabyte) of RAM to store its knowledge base and instructions. While AI can be done with a 16-bit microprocessor, which many home computers have, it works much faster and more efficiently with a 32-bit processor. However, AI programming languages and techniques can be modified for applications that, while not truly AI programs, have some of the beneficial traits of AI. "User-friendly" programs that allow a person to use familiar words and phrases rather than awkward computer commands, for example, are finally coming into their own, and the user-friendly Macintosh computer is very popular. Programs called "expert systems" are on the market and, while not expert systems in the AI sense, can be helpful.

Natural Language Understanding

A common complaint about personal computers is that they don't "understand" English as we use it. Before you can use most programs, you must learn their language. Programs from different companies use different commands, and switching among these various languages can be confusing and complicated. The Apple Macintosh computer and its imitators attempt to deal with this problem by having a "user-friendly interface" built into the computer. Software for these computers incorporates the helpful windows and other user-friendly features of the Macintosh into their programs so that people don't need to learn a new vocabulary and new techniques every time they purchase a program.

Dealing with more conventional computers, such as the IBM PC, is a different problem. The Natural Language Software Package from Safeguard Business Systems lets users handle customer accounts with simple English commands. When the computer doesn't understand, it queries back in conversational English rather than in "computerese." Savvy, from Excalibur, can create and change data using natural language, so it can store data on business inventories, prices, and so forth. Clout 2, a program from Microrim, allows people to use normal English, including synonyms, to get information from data base programs. For example, a user can tell Clout 2 that "people," "friends," and "persons" all mean the same as "name." If Clout 2 doesn't understand some words in a command such as "Give me the telephone numbers of people living in Chicago," it will tell you it doesn't know what "telephone numbers" are. You can then add that term to the list of synonyms for "phone." The program will then give you the numbers and will also respond correctly the next time you use the term "telephone numbers." With programs like Clout 2, a person can personalize software so that it "understands" language the way he or she uses it. Clout 2 also allows a user to pull together data stored in two different forms and then compare the information. Before, this sort of operation was impossible without knowledge of programming codes and plenty of time to write programs. Q & A, developed by Semantec, has an "Intelligent Assistant" that can understand such concepts as "and" and "or." It can search data files in response to natural queries such as "show all apartments with three bedrooms or two bedrooms and a den." Flexible, user-friendly programs like Clout 2 and Q & A will become more and more common for personal computers, and they owe a great deal to artificial intelligence techniques.

Expert Systems at Work and Home?

Most "expert systems" software produced for personal computers is quite different from a true expert system. For one thing, as we have seen, a home computer today doesn't have the memory or the disk storage space needed for a real expert system. An effective expert system is based on thousands of examples and on large numbers of factors to be weighed in making decisions.

The rules and an explanatory system also take up considerable amounts of memory. Even if small businesses and home users needed to develop their own customized expert systems, it would take months or years of interaction between an expert and a knowledge engineer. It is a very time-consuming and expensive process.

Most "expert systems" for personal computers are actually aids to decision-making, generally based on a "decision tree" format. The user fills in a selection of choices at the first set of branches, then at the next branch points, itemizing data that apply to each choice and giving a numerical score to each. For example, someone needs to buy a new car, but doesn't know which model would be best. With one of these "expert systems," he or she would make each car model one branch of the tree. The nodes produced from each of those branches contain the relevant information about the models—price, gas mileage, options, frequency of repair record, and so on. After all the data is filled in, the program will recommend the car that comes closest to meeting the stated needs. This sort of aid to decision-making may be useful in certain circumstances, but it is far from a true expert system. Things are changing fast, however. Expert system development tools for personal computers with lots of memory are now priced so that medium-sized businesses can afford them. Nextpert (from Neuron Data) runs on the 512K Macintosh. The user needs no knowledge of a programming language and works directly with the rules. A Texas Instruments program, Personal Consultant Plus, allows a personal computer user to develop an expert system in LISP. And Teknowledge's M.1 Version 2 can handle about a thousand rules. All these programs allow businesses to develop moderately large expert systems on computers they already own, without the need for a knowledge engineer.

Speech Recognition

Despite the difficulties (see Chapter 9), there are now simple and limited speech recognition systems. Some video games understand single word commands, and speech recognition hardware and software for personal computers is now available. The Votan speech board for the IBM PC allows the user to speak at conversational speed and be understood. The system must be "trained" to understand the voice of one person, who can customize personal word preferences such as "point" instead of "decimal." With this system, an executive who feels uncomfortable using a keyboard can speak instead, asking for particular information such as "current revenues" or "inventory count" from the computer.

At the Hope Center in Huntington Beach, California, the handicapped learn how to use computers to increase their independence. Gerald Schwartz, the president of the Hope Center, has written software enabling his students to use the Votan speech board and electrical connections to control electrical circuits that turn the lights off and on, water the lawn, or set the oven. The students can also control word processing and business programs by voice, which helps the writers and business professionals. As natural language understanding and voice recognition technologies improve, they will enable handicapped people to become increasingly self-reliant.

Games and AI

Computer games provide exciting potential for AI, especially as home computers become more powerful. Already, game writers are incorporating AI techniques to make their characters seem more "human." Chris Crawford, once a game creator with Atari, was inspired by AI in developing "Eastern Front." In this war game, the computer evaluates the advantages of different tactical maneuvers and chooses what looks like the best move. The data on the values of different moves are not stored as an AI-type tree but rather as a system of point values for each type of action—occupying a city, killing enemy soldiers, and the like.

"Incunabula," a multi-player game from Expert Systems, uses tree searches to determine the computer's responses to players' actions. Players choose the fundamental attitudes of their characters, and the actions of the computer are based on these attitudes. Because of the AI techniques incorporated into the program design, the characters have consistent, believable, but not completely predictable personalities, making the resulting game seem more "human."

Anyone who has played older adventure or fantasy games, in which commands must be typed into the computer, has probably encountered the frustration of not being understood by the machine. Using a word not in its vocabulary, or phrasing a command incorrectly, can bring the game to a standstill. In some games, it is impossible to continue without guessing and guessing until stumbling upon the "correct" command. Game designers are improving their parsers (see Chapter 6), using techniques borrowed from AI so that players can communicate more casually with the computer.

In a modern "interactive fiction" game, in which the player helps determine the outcome of the story, the parser has word tables listing all the command words that it understands. It has separate tables for nouns, verbs, prepositions, adjectives, and so on.

To see how the parser works, let's use a simple example with just a noun and a verb. You are playing an adventure game and have entered a castle room containing a chest. You type the command "examine chest." The parser compares "examine" and "chest" with the lists of words in its word tables to find matches. When it finds "examine" in the verb table, it assigns the word a number pair, say 1–8. After locating "chest" in the noun table, it assigns another number pair, such as 2–10. The first digit indicates the grammatical class of the word—"1" indicates a verb while "2" denotes a noun. Then, the number codes are sent to another part of the program, the "logic handler," which tries to make sense of the number pairs. If you typed in a nonsense command like "examine open," both number pairs would begin with a "1", indicating verbs, and the logic handler would reject them. If it receives a correct noun-verb set of pairs, it compares the set to number pairs in a table of all the possible commands in the game and the events that will result from those commands. If it finds a match, it returns the event number to the "event handler." The event handler checks the conditions of the game to make sure the command was appropriate, using "IF . . . THEN" statements. IF you are in the correct room based on your moves when you gave the command, THEN the program prints, YOU SEE A FABULOUS COLLECTION OF DAZZLINGLY SPARKLING JEWELS. But if you typed in "examine chest" and were in the king's chambers where there was no chest, the computer would respond with a comment like YOU CAN'T DO THAT HERE, or, with a more sophisticated parser, THERE IS NO CHEST HERE.

"Smart" parsers can also simplify communication with the game. For example, if you type in a command with no verb, a simple parser will respond with I CAN'T UNDERSTAND THAT or some similar comment. A smart one, however, will be able to tell you, THAT COMMAND IS MISSING A VERB. The more kinds of word tables representing parts of speech and the more different synonyms listed in the tables, the easier and more enjoyable the game is for the player. But the more information in the program, the more memory space it will take up, so "user-friendly" games require quite powerful computers. Thanks to AI techniques, however, the methods are there for making games more exciting.

Games of the Future

With interactive adventure games, "playing" on the computer is changing. The new adventures do more than just present puzzles. They allow the player to take on the personality of a character in the game and to see the imaginary world of the game through his or her eyes. A new "literary" experience is thus generated. When you read a book written from a character's viewpoint, you are observing the world through that character's eyes. But with a computer interactive adventure, you are actually participating as that character, not just observing. The two experiences are as different as watching a soccer game and playing in it.

Object-based languages are being used to write many of the new computer fiction adventures. As we saw in Chapter 5, these languages are naturals for dealing with objects and people. Some of the newer, more sophisticated parsers allow players to ask other characters questions such as "What would happen if I opened the door?" The response would depend on the way the question was phrased and on other factors. Penguin Software now uses a language called Comprehend, which features a full-sentence parser. This language makes it easier for professional writers to produce computer fiction, for they can write the material with a word processor. Comprehend carries out the work of translating the sentences into word tables for parsing.

Chris Crawford likes to compare the possibilities of computer fiction with that of other media. With the written word, for example, we start out as children reading comic books. When we get tired of them, we go on to novels written for children about horses, dogs, sports, or love. From there we can proceed to mass-market best-sellers about sex, power, and money. If we

"THIS IS NOT WHAT WE MEANT, SNIDER, WHEN WE ASKED FOR A THOROUGH STUDY OF THE LAWS OF GRAVITY."

Computer games hold fascination for people of all ages. Using AI techniques, games are becoming much more interesting and sophisticated.
Sidney Harris.

are truly interested in literature, there are enduring classics with depth of character and important observations about people and the world. The same sorts of levels exist for movies (for example, cartoons to teen films to grade B love/adventure stories to high-quality films) and even for food (for example, candy to fast-food to steak-and-seafood to gourmet classics). Crawford sees the same levels for computer literature. The arcade games have little depth, but are exciting and challenging on a physical level. Straight adventure and strategy games requiring some thought would perhaps represent the second level, while fantasy games in which the player must solve puzzles and build the attributes of his or her characters in order to succeed require still more sophistication. The newer interactive games, which make the player a fuller participant in their imaginary worlds, are a start toward the higher level of true computer "literature."

More memory and new technologies, such as laser disks, will help greatly in developing these games. And advances in AI techniques, especially in natural language understanding, will make vital contributions to the new computer literature. Until the player can freely participate in the game by typing in "natural language," there will always be a barrier between player and game. And if speech understanding develops to the point where a player could "speak" to the computer in natural language and have it understand and act on whatever he or she says, then even the artificial barrier of typing will be lifted. The player would then be an integrated and involved part of the game. The possibilities for true and deep creativity in such programs would be limitless.

12

Some More Problems for AI

AI research is full of excitement and surprises. No one suspected back in the 1950's where this intriguing field would lead. The relative ease of extracting expertise from a person with years of training and experience contrasts stunningly with the enormous difficulty of natural language understanding. AI research has now reached a sort of plateau. We know what the biggest problems are, according to experts like Roger Schank, but we don't yet know how to deal with them:

> The thing is, AI is very hard. What is the nature of knowledge? How do you abstract from existing knowledge to more general rules? How do you modify the knowledge when you fail? Are there principles of problem-solving that are independent of domain? How do goals and plans relate to understanding? The computer is a way of testing our ideas. But first, we need to understand what we're supposed to be building models of.

We must figure out how to endow computers with common sense and general knowledge and how to access those knowledge bases so that the computer "knows" when to use which facts.

We need ways of getting programs to learn from their own experience, as humans can, so that they can improve their performance over time. Perhaps no big breakthroughs will come using von Neumann machines, with their single microprocessors. It may be necessary to wait until computers with multiple processors and methods for programming them become well established. But meanwhile, it is important to recognize the bottlenecks and problems so that as the appropriate hardware becomes available, solutions can be found.

Another Look at Common Sense

Hubert Dreyfus, a philosopher at the University of California at Berkeley, has been a critic of AI since its early days. In 1972, Dreyfus wrote a book entitled *What Computers Can't Do* (revised in 1979), and has recently come out with *Mind Over Machine*, written with his brother Stuart. While his ideas and comments often annoy optimistic researchers, Dreyfus's doubts about current AI methods deserve attention, especially when they apply to a problem such as common sense. Dreyfus believes that AI researchers are going about common sense the wrong way. He doesn't think filling up computer memories with many pieces of information will ever solve this dilemma, for he does not regard common sense purely as a problem of knowledge:

> I think commonsense understanding isn't a kind of knowledge at all. . . . People don't have a lot of facts and rules in their minds for understanding the everyday world. They've got a kind of skill for coping with things. . . . This ability that people have to see what's relevant and to have the right thing pop into their head presupposes something like knowing what matters.

Dreyfus sees this idea of knowing what matters as being uniquely human; computers, in his view, can't have concern for what is happening or an understanding of the concept of "mattering." Without that sort of understanding, in his opinion, computers won't ever be able to exhibit commonsense reasoning. He also believes that common sense involves many complex aspects of brain functioning—recalling memories or stored images and finding similarities in things which may not share obvious qualities or quantities. For example, the way you feel when you hear a particular song may remind you of your thoughts at an earlier time when you saw a special photograph. Your interpretation of the song may be influenced by recollections with no overt connection to the music at all. A computer could not react in this way, for, in order to analyze a situation, it must break the input down into its individual features. It cannot respond to the whole and find overall similarities.

To Dreyfus, "Common sense includes feelings, having a body, having images, responding to similarities, etc.," and lists of facts and rules just cannot get at the essence of common sense. He believes that, as long as AI researchers persist in using the approach of listing pieces of commonsense knowledge in logic programs, arranging them as terminals of frames or components of scripts, they will never get a computer to understand a story even as well as a four-year-old child. Dreyfus does have hope for the future, however, if programs can be developed that come closer to simulating the way the brain actually works. Such an approach probably won't get very far with present-day computers, because it would have to simulate effectively the three-dimensional nature of neural networks and the variable strength of some nerve impulses.

How Humans Acquire Language and Common Sense

The intellectual skills and knowledge of humans far surpass those of any other living things on earth, and the time from birth to adulthood in humans also greatly exceeds that of other creatures, even in proportion to life span. These two facts are probably related. There is so much for a person to learn that he or she needs years to do it. The newborn human is very helpless. All it can do is suck to get nourishment and cry to attract attention to its needs. But right from the start, the infant begins observing its world, trying to focus its uncoordinated eyes on nearby objects and listening to the sounds in its environment. Psychologists are just beginning to realize how aware babies are of their environment and how much they quickly come to understand about it.

As the infant grows, it learns to control its body, first to reach out with its hands to grab at objects and then to crawl. Usually by the time it is 18 months old, a baby can walk and speak a few words. The details of how children learn language are almost unknown. "Baby talk" often imitates the rhythm of the native language they hear around them. At around one year of age, a baby learns a few words, and by the time it is about two- to two-and-a-half years old, the child begins to put words together into sentences. A three-year-old knows over a thousand words to make sentences and communicate quite effectively with other humans. The child can produce original sentences that he or she has never heard before, and the sentences are usually properly constructed.

It may seem amazing that in three years a child goes from being a helpless baby that can communicate only by crying, to an original speaker who can express complex language. But when we look at the situation from the viewpoint of programming a computer, three years is a long time!

A tremendous amount of energy goes into learning to communicate with words as, simultaneously, the young child is also observing the world and trying to make sense of it. While a three-year-old has some commonsense knowledge, there is still a great deal to learn. This lack of mastery of the world is part of what makes young children so charming. Their language often sounds so grown-up, yet their ideas about how the world works can be very amusing to an older child or an adult.

Psychologists often divide childhood into stages which, they theorize, are related to the development and maturation of the brain. And certainly, the brain does grow and change as a child grows up. But there may be more to the stages of development than the physical side. Scientists struggling with AI programs have discovered that every normal human has an enormous amount of commonsense knowledge and a great mastery of the subtleties of language. Maybe a major reason it takes a human being so long to grow up and understand his or her world is that there is such an incredible amount to learn before achieving an adult level of understanding.

Perhaps we are asking too much of computers. We are expecting adult human beings to create a program with the language mastery, judgment, and ability to deal with the world that took the same humans many years of learning and experience to acquire. And we expect the computer to store and utilize this information with hardware almost infinitely simpler than that nature gave to the human being.

The Problem of Learning

Finding effective ways for AI programs to learn is crucial in developing sophisticated programs and in keeping expert systems up-to-date. As we have just seen, it takes years for a human to learn enough to function smoothly in society. Unless we can produce computer programs that can learn, we are unlikely ever to have machines that exhibit true generalized intelligence. "Learning" actually refers to a variety of phenomena and situations. We learn by acquiring new information from books or from listening to other people talk; we learn by being told how to accomplish a task and then by practicing; and we learn by figuring things out for ourselves—by applying different rules and ideas to a problem until we come up with a solution. Perhaps the information that sticks with us best is the kind we pick up by doing, by solving problems, and by trial-and-error effort.

How do AI researchers define learning? Herbert Simon uses a general definition—learning is "any process by which a system improves its performance." This definition requires a task to perform and assumes that the system can improve its performance—that is, learn—by applying new techniques or new knowledge or by improving on existing methods.

A more limited definition of learning is "the acquisition of skills." This definition applies both to actual physical skills, such as those that would be performed and improved by robots, and to mental skills, such as problem-solving. It emphasizes learning by doing. Knowledge engineers and others concerned with expert systems are especially interested in learning as the acquisition of specific knowledge. They need ways to get a system to acquire new knowledge and new rules easily and to integrate them into the knowledge and rules already present in the system. Without this ability, an expert system becomes rapidly outdated and soon useless.

A final definition of learning involves deriving general rules and theories from knowledge given. This is the method of science—take facts and develop a hypothesis that explains them, or deduce general laws from specific examples. If computers could master this sort of learning, they could indeed be powerful, with their ability to retain detail and their potential for keeping many different facts in the forefront at one time. If a computer were able to develop hypotheses, it could test them against a great number of facts much more rapidly than a person could.

Programs That Learn

In Chapter 8 we saw the effectiveness of rote learning in Samuel's checkers program. Once the program had looked ahead at a particular sequence of moves, it stored the knowledge so that the next time that sequence was possible, it could retrieve the backed-up value instead of recalculating it. With this method, the more the program played, the better it became at playing, for the program could "see" further and further ahead in the game. Rote learning, however, can be effective only in a very limited domain.

Edward Feigenbaum of Stanford University sees the problem of learning as crucial to the development of expert systems and other programs that should exhibit common sense:

> What makes commonsense reasoning so difficult is that you need to know so many facts about the world. How many facts? A million? . . . But who's going to take the time to codify all that? . . . What it's going to take is

hoards of graduate students working for a generation. That's why the dream of AI since 1955 or 1956 has been to write a program that can learn from experience. That's the right approach—if only we knew how to do it.

The problem of computer learning is being tackled in a number of laboratories. A program called FOO, developed by D. J. Mostow, plays the card game Hearts and can integrate advice from a person into its procedures. FOO is able to reorganize the advice into a form that it can use in playing the game. For example, in Hearts, the goal is to achieve as low a score as possible; thus, the players try to avoid taking points. When the human designer of the program tells FOO, in an appropriate computer language statement, that it should "avoid taking points," FOO must reorganize this information into a statement about how to play its own cards. When actually playing, FOO formulates hypotheses about the best cards to play to keep its score low, applying appropriate heuristics, since it doesn't know which cards are in the opponents' hands.

EURISKO, developed by Douglas Lenat of Stanford and his students, can use general heuristics to discover new principles.

Edward Feigenbaum of Stanford University is at the forefront of work in expert systems. He believes that developing programs that can learn from experience is the key to success in AI research.

Courtesy of the Department of Computer Science, Stanford University.

Researchers give EURISKO knowledge about a specific domain, such as computer programming or the cleanup of chemical spills, and the program analyzes the facts and comes to its own conclusions. EURISKO has hundreds of general heuristics, such as "look at extreme cases," which guide its exploration of a new field of knowledge. The methods it uses are the same type used by scientists. EURISKO has an important advantage over many AI programs. It is designed so that it can spend hours on its own, examining the information it is given, deriving hypotheses about the data, and coming to conclusions. While most computer programs do not keep records of their activities as they run, EURISKO does. In this way, it can apply a principle it derived while working on one kind of data to another type of problem.

Integrating new knowledge into expert systems can be very tricky. A new rule may conflict with an old one already in the system, or it may be stated too generally and then mistakenly called up in situations where a specific rule was more appropriate. There are many such problems in developing expert systems and keeping them up-to-date. Ultimately, a system that could check for inconsistencies, find bugs, and ask the expert how to eliminate a bug would save a lot of time for knowledge engineers and experts alike. A start has been made. Programs for developing expert systems, such as EMYCIN, do have functions that alert developers to difficulties in integrating knowledge. This makes putting an expert system together and keeping it up-to-date more efficient.

Storing and Accessing Knowledge

We have seen that storing knowledge in an AI program so it can be appropriately accessed is crucial. Many researchers believe that developing effective ways of storing and retrieving knowledge is the key to successful AI programming. For many reasons, the problem is a complex one.

First of all, there is the sheer volume of information necessary for natural language understanding and commonsense knowledge. Ways must be found to store that knowledge compactly, to take up as little memory as possible.

A far more difficult problem, however, is arranging the knowledge so that it is brought to bear whenever appropriate. Some knowledge is so general that it must almost always be kept in mind, while other facts apply only to certain situations. Often, information will be applicable to an assortment of situations that do not seem to be related. Facts about color, for example, would be vital to understanding a variety of situations—landscapes, clothing, interior decoration, animal breeds, and so on. The brain can instantly pull out relevant information without searching through its entire memory. When more is known about how the brain functions and when the new generation of computers is fully developed, perhaps a way will be found to achieve the same feat through computers. Until then, machines that are truly "intelligent," in the sense that an average human is, will not exist.

13

New Hardware,
New Plans

AI progress is limited with the von Neumann machine, but new designs that utilize many microprocessors are appearing. Current expert systems, even in the biggest, fastest computers, can have only a few thousand rules and a restricted knowledge base; simple robots are still painfully slow. One robot capable of using a computer visual system to wend its way down a hallway full of obstacles has to stop for 15 minutes every yard or so to reevaluate its progress. The more computing done with a serial system, the longer it takes for the data to pass through the bottleneck created by the single processor. It's like a supermarket on a Saturday afternoon with only one checkout counter open. The brain is about a million times slower than microchip circuits, but operations that take an instant for the brain with the simultaneous functioning of its neurons take minutes with a computer.

There are many different ways of designing computers with parallel processors. Some already exist, such as the Cray-1 supercomputer on which the Cray Blitz chess program runs and the champion chess machine Hitech (see Chapter 8). The Cosmic Cube, developed at the California Institute of Technology, is a relatively small computer for business and science that links together in a complex network 64 processors, each with its own memory. Computers like the Cray-1 and the Cosmic Cube, how-

"SURE IT'S DEPRESSING. THIS THING HAS A MEMORY OF 3 TRILLION BITS, AND I CAN'T RECALL WHAT I HAD FOR LUNCH."

While increased memory enables computers to store more information and look at more alternatives, it is not the solution to better AI programs.
Sidney Harris.

ever, were designed to increase the speed of processing for solving problems in physical science and mathematics, where problems involve the same equations over and over again. They are essentially super-number-crunchers. But AI problems must be dealt with in a loose and flexible way; rigidity won't work, so other designs will probably prove more useful for AI.

The Fifth Generation

Just which computers will turn out to be best for AI remains to be seen. New machines, with an organization different from the von Neumann design of the first computer generations, have been dubbed the "Fifth Generation." Because Japan is so boldly plunging into the new technology, that term has come to refer more to Japan's efforts than any others.

The ten-year Fifth Generation project was announced by the Japanese in October 1981. The Japanese government allocated $450 million to develop new hardware and new software for "intelligent" computers, and the private companies that will carry out the work are contributing about $400 million more. They have a variety of impressive goals and 24 different projects for developing computer systems devoted to AI. Before the Fifth Generation, AI was implemented only on machines designed for other kinds of work. The Japanese, however, are developing computers with "logic processors" that handle logic the way current processors handle machine language code. Instead of working with numbers, the logic processors deal with symbolic calculations. A modification of PROLOG (see Chapter 5) is the "machine language" of the new computers. As Edward Feigenbaum points out, most of the important problems in the world are solved not by mathematical calculation, but rather by inference. People do not usually think mathematically—they think using reason. Computers that could do the same will be enormously more powerful and helpful than those that are basically numerical.

Among other things, the Japanese want to get their new machines to process logic faster than present computers work with numbers. The speed of computers is calculated as "arithmetic operations per seconds," which currently runs into the millions. The computers planned by the Japanese will carry out logic inferences (steps in IF . . . THEN statements) at speeds measured in "logic inferences per seconds," abbreviated LIPS. The Japanese hope to develop machines capable of performing a billion LIPS—called a gigilips—by 1991. To achieve this speed, parallel processors will be essential, as will chips packed with an impressive density of transistors. Chips that can store a million bits now exist, but the Japanese are aiming for ones capable of storing ten times as much information.

The architecture of the Fifth Generation machines will be completely different from that of today's computers. The Japanese are tackling all aspects of intelligent machines, too—designing and organizing the knowledge base, perfecting rule bases and their implementation, and devising user-friendly interfaces.

The Japanese also want to store knowledge bases containing a hundred million objects (in the sense used in the language Smalltalk, see Chapter 5) and tens of thousands of rules. Such a powerful machine could store the contents of a large encyclopedia. Another goal is to develop a machine translation program between English and Japanese that would have a vocabulary of 100,000 words and would translate with an accuracy of around 90 percent. A speech understanding program is also in the works. It would have a 50,000-word vocabulary and would ultimately be able to comprehend continuous human speech by a few hundred different speakers with 95 percent accuracy. Not only that, it would operate a voice-activated typewriter and talk back to its users in either English or Japanese, using a synthesized voice. Fifth Generation machines would also be able to understand maps and photographs as well as words.

What Is at Stake

If the Japanese accomplish their goals, they could corner the market on important new technologies necessary in the modern age. "Knowledge is power," and systems for storing and manipulating knowledge add to that power. The Japanese live on crowded islands with few natural resources, so they rely on their human resources in the international marketplace. Intelligent machines would be sought by all sorts of businesses around the world, and the manufacture of those machines would be extremely important in the world economy.

Some European countries, and the United States, have responded to the Japanese challenge by proposing plans of their own for new technology. The European Strategic Program for Research and Development in Information Technology (ESPRIT) is allocating $2.6 billion over ten years to Fifth Generation development, and Great Britain has come up with a five-year $300 million program to share the costs of developing an intelligent computer with universities and industry. A dozen American companies have gotten together and organized the Microelectronics and Computer Technology Corporation (MCC). The MCC has a central laboratory in Austin, Texas, staffed mostly by company employees on loan for four years. Most of the research takes place there rather than in the laboratories of the individual companies.

The United States military's Defense Advanced Research Projects Agency (DARPA), which has been funding AI research for many years, is trying to meet the need for new technologies with a $1 billion Strategic Computing program. In addition to research in the general areas of AI and in developing parallel processing technologies, the Strategic Computing program has three specific goals: a system for managing naval battles through complex graphics, a pilot's aid that would respond to spoken commands to help fly the plane and determine strategy, and a driverless land vehicle that could move over varied terrain and seek cover to hide itself from possible enemies. The DARPA research is being done both by universities and by private industry.

Finding the Best Design

There is a real problem in designing these systems—developing hardware is difficult without knowing something about the type of software to be used, and designing software is impossible without knowledge of the hardware! Some AI workers, as a matter of fact, do not feel it is time yet to design new hardware. They think we should solve some of the questions about representing knowledge, imparting common sense, and getting computers to learn, before we begin developing new hardware. Says Roger Schank:

> First we need to understand what we're building models of. If we could build a machine that could function correctly, but slowly, THEN parallel processing might have something to say.

Other researchers, however, believe that faster processors will make it easier to test ideas about designing intelligent systems. Results that take weeks with current machines could be obtained in minutes or seconds using parallel processors.

Allen Newell of Carnegie-Mellon University believes that different computer architectures, such as parallel processors, and the new ways of programming that would go with them, could stimulate our thinking about intelligence. "We aren't smart enough to change our thinking without that kind of challenge," says Newell. His colleague Geoffrey Hinton agrees:

> There has been a long-standing split in AI, those who say you don't need to worry about the hardware in AI, just the data structures and so forth—that is the approach that has led to expert systems and all the success in the marketplace—and a much less influential school (so far) who say that the kind of hardware available determines the kind of problems you can do well.

Although Hinton realizes that new computer designs will stimulate new kinds of programming, he is reluctant to jump into producing new hardware too soon:

> It's a paradox. People are using conventional computers to simulate the parallel ideas. It's very slow, and eventually we'll have to build parallel systems. But until we know how to do the proper kind of programming, it's too early—we wouldn't know what kind of parallel system to build.

Hinton himself is experimenting with parallel programming ideas. One very promising design is called the BOLTZMANN architecture, named for the nineteenth-century physicist Ludwig Boltzmann. A BOLTZMANN machine would have memory spread through a system with many small processors. It would be able to take new information and combine it with stored memory to come up with a solution in a reasonable amount of time. The technology allows the machine to search all its hypotheses at the same time so that it doesn't get bogged down in the magnitude of the search. It also enables a solution to be found even when the data is incomplete. Hinton likes to use the example of a tiger hiding in a jungle. When a lone human gets a glimpse of even the tiger's tail, he or she immediately knows a number of things—there is a tiger there, it could be dangerous, I should get away, and so on. The brain doesn't spend a lot of time trying to make sense of the scene; it can extract the important information, relate it to memory, and act upon it—all in an instant. Hinton is hopeful that programs can be developed using BOLTZMANN architecture which could take the image of the tail and match it up not only with "tiger," but also with "danger," "run," and so forth.

Experimental Hardware

At least a dozen different parallel computers are in the works. Many issues must be considered in drawing up plans for computers with parallel processors. The size of the individual processors themselves is an important question. The systems now in use, such as the Cosmic Cube, use large processors like those found in conventional computers. One new AI computer, developed at Columbia University and dubbed DADO, has 1023 small individual processors. DADO is designed for running expert systems and works about ten times as fast as ordinary machines.

Because AI so often requires that small amounts of data be examined in several different and flexible ways at a time, some new machines use many very small processors, sometimes so small that a large number can be etched onto the same VLSI chip. This approach attempts to produce computers closer in architecture to the human brain in hopes that brainlike function will be easier to develop with brainlike structure. NON VON (for non-von Neumann), another Columbia design, will ultimately have a million tiny processors, each with its own small bit of memory. That memory would contain a single element of data. Since each element would have its own processor, the computer would behave as if each piece of data could itself do work.

Another problem is how to join multiple processors together. Should they all be connected in some way to one another, or should they be arranged in a different way—say, in a circle? When there are thousands of processors, it is very difficult to connect them all. The processors of both NON VON and DADO are arranged in a treelike system that mirrors the structure of so many AI problems. In NON VON, there will also be larger processors linked to the small ones in the first few levels of the tree, down to about where there are 256 processors. The larger ones could do their own work or send signals to the smaller processors to which they are linked. In addition, the large processors will all be interconnected so they can share information with one another. The design of NON VON allows the computer to have a million processors and still have some communication among the parts of the system.

In the Connection Machine, being developed by W. Daniel Hillis of Thinking Machines Corporation, in Waltham, Massachusetts, each of the million processors will be able to communicate with every other one. This feat will be accomplished by designing chips containing 64 tiny processors each. The million-processor machine will have 16,384 of these chips, all connected as if there were vertices of an imaginary "hypercube" in 14-dimensional space! Chips arranged in this way could communicate with one another much more quickly than if they were joined more conventionally. Hillis' goal in developing the Connection Machine is to produce a computer capable of "behaving" as intelligently as a six-year-old person, what he calls an "amateur system," as opposed to an "expert system."

How can a million or more processors be coordinated and controlled? Should there be a centralized system that parcels out the work to the individual units, or should each processor be on its own? Central control provides a system more like a familiar von Neumann machine, but perhaps decentralized computers would be better at making logical inferences from large knowledge bases. With no central control, each processor must store its own program in its own individual memory, so the processors must be bigger than in centralized machines such as NON VON. While at least some American designs use central control, the Japanese have chosen decentralized architecture for their Fifth Generation machines.

Artificial intelligence is beginning a new era, with new hardware so much more powerful than what is currently available that it is difficult to predict what will come next. With greater "intelligence," these computers will have greater power over human problems and over people themselves. Considering *now* the relationships of such computers to people is important, so that we will be somewhat prepared for their influence in the future.

14

AI and the
Human Mind and Spirit

What implications does AI have for human culture? What light has it shed on the concept of "intelligence"? What effects might intelligent machines have on society and on the human spirit? While people are intrigued by the idea of computers that think, they are also frightened. Ever since Samuel's checkers program in the early 1960's, humans have been nervous about computers. Officials at IBM, Samuel's employer at the time, went out of their way to downplay his program. It seemed too much like "machine thinking," and the company didn't want to alarm people about the new technology. Now philosophers wonder if thinking machines will devalue the human mind and turn us into mere biological robots. They are concerned about the problems associated with having "intelligent" machines making important decisions, especially military ones.

What Is Human Intelligence?

In Chapter 1 we chose to use a definition of artificial intelligence that avoided the question, "What is intelligence?" Now that we have surveyed the field and evaluated the problems and possibilities, it is time to reexamine this question.

"IT WAS BOUND TO HAPPEN — THEY'RE BEGINNING TO THINK LIKE BINARY COMPUTERS."

What effects will increasing use of computers have on future generations? (By the way, the boy has found the correct answer.)
Sidney Harris.

AI research has shown that the concept of intelligence is quite confused. Traditional IQ tests, which are supposed to measure relative intelligence, rely on the ability to solve verbal and mathematical problems quickly. For many years, critics of IQ tests have argued that they test only a narrow part of what constitutes true intelligence. IQ tests ignore creativity, for example, which many would argue is a more important part of intelligence than the ability to solve mathematical problems rapidly. They also ignore artistic ability, communication skills, and other talents that allow people to function intelligently.

Society has always regarded as particularly intelligent those who are talented in mathematics and those who have mastered one area of knowledge, especially a field such as medicine, which has high prestige in our culture. A good memory and the ability to think fast have traditionally been a part of the definition of great intelligence. Now, however, we have discovered that exactly these two traits are the easiest to duplicate with machines! Computers have a much more reliable memory than humans, and a computer can carry out calculations at far greater speed than the human brain.

Does this mean that computers are naturally more intelligent than people? Some might think so, but AI research has taught us that true intelligence involves much more than fast thinking and a good memory. How can we call a machine "intelligent" when it doesn't even know it is a machine, when it has no concept of the world that created it, and when it doesn't have sense enough to come in out of the rain? In defining intelligence in the past, people have taken so much of the human mind for granted. They have set the "average" adult human as a baseline from which to measure this elusive trait, taking for granted the remarkable abilities that allow a human even to be "average."

The discoveries of AI should not make people feel less special because machines can do some of the things humans have always equated with braininess. Quite the contrary. AI work has shown that even a person of less-than-average intelligence by traditional measures has an amazing store of information and knows how to use it to survive in a complicated world.

Can Machines Think?

Programs like SHRDLU and expert systems are able to examine information and come to conclusions. One of the major goals of AI research is to develop programs that are better and better at this sort of activity, which many would define as "thinking." So the question arises, "Can machines think?" Some would say yes, some would say no, and others would say we should wait and see. While the question of machine thought is an interesting one that can provoke plenty of discussion, Seymour Papert (the inventor of LOGO; see Chapter 5), has a very clear-eyed and useful way of examining the question:

> Obviously, people don't think the same way as machines. People are biological. When we ask if a machine thinks, we are asking whether we would like to extend the notion of thinking to include what machines might do. That is the only meaningful sense of the question: Do machines think?

Papert believes, clearly, that what machines do when they come to conclusions is very different from what humans do. However, he also feels that it is important not to dismiss the kind of "thinking" carried out by machines:

> AI, if it's going to be taken seriously, is introducing a new technical concept of thinking, one that is not the same as the concept of thinking that's existed since Aristotle and before.

What Is the Mind?

One of the great philosophical questions is, "What is the mind?" This question is really separate from those about intelligence and thinking, for the mind encompasses the totality of what we believe makes humans unique. Most scientists would probably say that the mind is nothing more than the manifestation of brain function, especially of the cerebral cortex. Many religions link the mind with the human soul. Here, we will look at the mind in a somewhat different way. We know that it is difficult to get a machine to exhibit true, generalized intelligence. But if it proves possible, would that machine have a mind?

The British scientist A. Sloman looks upon the mind as a mechanism that specializes in acquiring, building, storing, and using symbols. AI workers are trying to develop just such mechanisms with their programs. But the mind is not like a computer and its program, for the mind handles symbols in a particular way—a human way. How we filter, classify, and use the input from our environment and how we convert it all into symbols has to do with what it means to be human. It involves our uniquely human sensory system; we are not able to perceive all the potential input, for our sense organs are limited. We cannot see ultraviolet light as bees can, for example, nor can we hear extremely high-pitched sounds like dogs can.

The need to keep the body alive and well slants our interpretation of the environment, while a computer needn't "worry" about such things. Humans have a great social need—the vast majority of us are not happy unless we have some social contact with other humans, and many of our mental traits are related to the social nature of people. Computers do not have this need.

From this point of view, much of what constitutes the mind is related to what it means to be human. It involves not only thinking and learning, it concerns emotions, needs, desires, ideals, dislikes, and so on. It takes into account the effects of our actions on other humans and requires us to compromise in order to satisfy all our conflicting thoughts, needs, and feelings. When we think of the mind in this way, the computer begins to look very "simpleminded."

Can Computers Have Emotions?

If we want computers to be more like humans, maybe we should somehow endow them with emotions. Is this possible? Would it be a good idea? The founders of AI disagree about computers and emotions. John McCarthy feels there is no point in having a computer with emotions, even if we could produce one. After all, humans often have trouble making decisions and dealing with life because of their conflicting emotions. What good would an angry computer be? Lack of emotion, in this view, is definitely an advantage of computers in decision-making.

Marvin Minsky, on the other hand, thinks we can and perhaps should program emotions into computers. He believes that people actually understand emotions better than they understand thinking. We have trouble describing our thought processes, but we are more adept at analyzing emotion. If you ask a man, for example, why he is mad at his wife, he may say that he really isn't angry with her, it's just that the boss was mean to him and he can't take it out on the boss, so he takes it out on his wife instead. But if you asked the same man how he came up with a new idea at the office, he would probably tell you that it just "popped into" his head.

Indeed, emotions may be necessary in a computer to make it more intelligent. If our goal is to produce a computer that can function intelligently in the real world, emotions may be a necessary component. As Sloman puts it:

> The possibility of having emotions may be a by-product of being able to cope with a complex and partly unpredictable world in an intelligent way.

What Is Consciousness?

The ultimate question in comparing computers and humans is, "Can computers ever be conscious beings?" John Searle, a philosopher at the University of California at Berkeley, thinks that consciousness is a key issue in the comparison. He believes that a computer can never think like a human because it cannot have mental states. He describes the following scenario as a way of looking at the question:

Suppose there is a man isolated in a room. He is given a list of rules on how to manipulate the symbols of the Chinese writing system. The man doesn't know the Chinese language, but the rules for shuffling the symbols around are so good that he can produce perfectly grammatical Chinese in response to questions in Chinese. When he is given a question, he looks up the rules for manipulating the symbols to produce a correct response. If he is asked, "Do you understand Chinese?" he manipulates the symbols to produce a response such as "Of course I do!"

The man in the room in Searle's hypothetical example is like a computer. He knows how to manipulate the symbols, but he really doesn't know what they mean. Thus, according to Searle, no matter how well a computer performs, it lacks the quality

"THE BEAUTY OF THIS SYSTEM IS THAT THERE ARE A FEW SMALL ERRORS PROGRAMMED INTO IT, WHICH HELPS TO AVOID TOTAL DEPERSONALIZATION."

Will we have to produce computers that make errors in order to get them to be more "human"?
Sidney Harris.

of understanding associated with consciousness. The manipulation of symbols according to formal rules, no matter how sophisticated, does not produce meaning. To Searle, the computer is not on its way to having a mind because it hasn't even gotten started in that direction; it is not the business of a computer to have a mind.

There is opposition to Searle's scenario. John McCarthy offers the following criticism:

> He makes no distinction . . . between the hardware (the person) and the process (the set of rules). I would argue that the set of rules understands Chinese, and, analogously, a computer program may be said to understand things, even if a computer does not.

McCarthy makes an important point in distinguishing between the hardware and the process. The rules do, in their own way, understand Chinese. But the fact that the computer does not can be construed as an argument in favor of Searle's viewpoint. McCarthy is actually agreeing that the computer lacks consciousness, since he agrees that it does not "understand" anything.

An important distinction between the mind and a computer is that the computer acts only in response to the things to which it is programmed to respond, whereas the human mind functions autonomously. When a person types a question or problem into a computer, the program is activated to produce an answer. When the visual or sound-sensing capabilities of a computer or robot are turned on and the machine is instructed to analyze the input, it does so. The computer needs data or queries as "food," or it cannot function. But the human mind cannot be turned off and on at will. It is constantly active. We are capable of, even driven to carry out, independent thought. If you lie down in a silent, dark room, you continue to think, despite the limited sensory input. As a matter of fact, you may get some of your best ideas and insights in just that condition, with minimum external stimulation and your mind free to "do its own thing." If you are tired and fall asleep, still your mind doesn't turn off.

It produces dreams, imaginative concoctions mixing reality with fantasy that can sometimes tell you a great deal about yourself and your feelings.

This constant awareness and analysis that goes on in our minds is perhaps the essence of consciousness, and it clearly is something computers lack. Without instructions from their human "masters," computers just sit and wait.

Another aspect of consciousness is introspection—the ability to think about oneself. For example, we can think about the questions introduced in this chapter, which are philosophical. On the other hand, a computer cannot and perhaps never will be able to do so. Such questions as "What is thought?", "What is the mind?", and "What is consciousness?" require consciousness to investigate and, at this time, consciousness seems to be beyond the capabilities of the computer, no matter how sophisticated.

How People View Intelligent Computers

People tend to overestimate the capabilities of computers. When Joseph Weizenbaum saw the reaction to his program ELIZA, he was shocked into writing an entire book entitled *Computer Power and Human Reason*. People were all too willing to look upon ELIZA as something more than a clever computer program. As Weizenbaum recounts:

> I was startled to see how quickly and how very deeply people conversing with [ELIZA] became emotionally involved with the computer and how unequivocally they anthropomorphized it. Once my secretary, who had watched me work on the program for many months and therefore surely knew it to be merely a computer program, started conversing with it. After only a few interchanges with it, she asked me to leave the room. Another time, I suggested I might rig the system so that I could examine all conversations anyone had with it, say, overnight. I was promptly bombarded with accusations that what I proposed amounted to spying on people's most intimate thoughts; clear evidence that people were conversing with the computer as if it were a person who could be appropriately and usefully addressed in intimate terms.

Weizenbaum was also upset to read accounts by psychologists touting ELIZA as a forebear of a computer that could take over for human therapists, and by others proclaiming that the program was a general solution to the problem of understanding natural language. In his book, Weizenbaum struggles with the question of why people are so ready to accept machines as all-powerful.

As computer jargon becomes more and more a part of our lives, people are using it to describe their own functioning. We talk about our misunderstandings as "bugs," and, when we need to learn how to perform a task, we may say that we have to be "programmed" for it. Some people fear that this sort of attitude indicates an increasing willingness to view ourselves merely as sophisticated machines. To these people, the goals of AI are dehumanizing and the field should, perhaps, not even be pursued. They fear that as computers become more adept at mimicking people, people will become less and less human themselves.

Joseph Weizenbaum worries that people are too willing to accept without question the expertise of computers.
The MIT Museum.

Terry Winograd of Stanford University is concerned with the moral aspects of AI research, especially when it is applied to military uses.
Courtesy of the News and Publications Service, Stanford University.

Making Decisions

With computers being programmed to take over more and more of the decision-making in our society, these questions become increasingly important. It is crucial always to keep in mind that computers and robots are man-made machines, their capabilities set by humans and their circuits made of silicon and metal, not living flesh. Just what sorts of computers we design and what tasks we assign to them are important social and moral responsibilities that need to be discussed and considered very seriously.

A great number of people are concerned about the future roles of computers in society. Terry Winograd worries that, by developing computers that can do so much, we are creating systems with no ultimate human responsibility:

> We are setting up ways of understanding, ways of working with computer systems that create a forgetfulness about responsibility. The whole area of

computers and intelligence leads to people dealing with systems where, in some sense or the other, it is taken for granted . . . that no person is actually involved, that somehow the system is doing it.

This problem is especially serious when it comes to the military applications of AI. The vast majority of AI research in the United States is funded by the military, through DARPA. The goals of the Strategic Computing program include developing robots that will have great influence over military activities and decisions. "Star wars" space weapons technology will also involve advances made by AI researchers. As Winograd says, speaking of AI researchers:

We cannot hide from the fact that information technology plays as great a role in nuclear forces as does nuclear physics technology and rocket technology. . . . We too design the machines of nuclear war. That means we have moral responsibilities that can hardly be exaggerated.

Paul Smolensky of the University of California at Irvine shares Winograd's concern. He points out that the military is rushing to use computers in key roles in the arms race without taking into consideration the computers' considerable limitations. We know that programming computers to perform in complex, flexible human situations is extremely difficult, yet military AI applications will involve international politics, and one mistake could lead to catastrophe.

Understanding Ourselves

The field of artificial intelligence is still young, and there is a great deal left to learn. Much of what we have found out already, however, has shed light on what it means to be human. It has shown us that being human is very complicated and that "intelligence" is not what we thought it was. The abilities of the ordinary person are now seen to be quite amazing, while the accomplishments of the expert seem less overwhelming. When Turing wrote his influential paper in 1950, he felt that by the year 2000, there would be a computer good enough at imitating a person that, after five minutes of questioning, an interrogator would have a 30 percent chance of guessing wrong about which subject was the computer in the Turing Test. This sounds like a conservative estimate, but Marvin Minsky believes that it will be at least 300 years before we can program a computer to make a decent showing in the Turing Test.

Why are we such a long way from a computer that seems human? The key appears to be that a computer will never be a human. The mind of a person is more than a collection of neurons. It is the sum total of all the shared and unique experiences of the person's life. At any given moment, the mind is also the sum total of the influences being exerted by the environment and the physiological state of the body in which it resides. Not only does the sensory input from the environment affect the mind, so do the chemical influences within the body. Hormones (chemicals that affect the responses of cells, including neurons), energy level (tired or ready to go), state of satisfaction (hungry or full, thirsty or not)—all these factors have a tremendous influence on how we experience the world at any given moment.

The human mind must be seen as a whole, for it functions that way. Because of its ability to integrate all its influences, the mind can take many details and fuse them together into the "big picture" without conscious thought. We have seen that chess champions do not laboriously go through thousands of possible moves as the computer must, and that expert scientists can identify the type of problem and see its solution without running through lists of rules. Scientists wonder how we can get computers to do this. While they may try, the question remains: can we do it at all?

Humans may just be too complex to capture in a machine. Terry Winograd now works at the Center for the Study of Language and Information at Stanford University. The center was founded in 1983 and brings together workers from many language-related fields: psychology, linguistics, philosophy, and computer science. They hope that by combining their resources they can learn more about the roots of language and language understanding. But, as Winograd believes, this is a tall order. According to him, the idea that language and thought can be modeled by formal logic or similar methods is much too simplistic. He feels that the key to language is its social context and that what goes on when people talk together is so deeply rooted that it is mostly unconscious and cannot be communicated to the computer:

> What people actually do has very little in common with formal logic. . . . And what's missing is the social dimension. Once you take into account what you are using a word for, what part it plays in discourse, there is no boundary to the meaning of that word.

If Winograd is correct, computers will never be copies of human beings, no matter how "intelligent" we can make them. The social aspects of language, the myriad subtleties of meaning that particular words have to each individual person, can never be captured in silicon and metal. Humans will always retain their unique humanity, even when their superior minds have been able to provide computers with some semblance of human thought.

Glossary

algorithm A fixed procedure that will come up with a solution to a problem.

any-path problem A problem for which the route to a solution doesn't matter as long as a solution is reached.

backed-up value A numerical value in a game program calculated by the computer after it has looked several moves ahead.

backtracking A method of search that starts with a possible solution and works backward through the search tree. Also called backward chaining.

best-path problem A problem in which it is necessary to find the best path to the solution.

binary system A number system based on the number 2. (The system we commonly use is the decimal system, based on the number 10.)

bit The smallest quantity of information used by a computer, which is a 0 or a 1 in binary. (Bit stands for BInary digiT.)

bug A flaw in a program.

byte A string of eight bits. Most computers take in information in byte-sized chunks.

combinatorial explosion A frequent problem in AI work, resulting from the vast number of combinations possible when large numbers of alternatives are involved.

DARPA The U.S. military's Defense Advanced Research Projects Agency, which funds most of the AI research in the United States.

expert system A computer system that incorporates the knowledge of an expert or experts in a given realm, such as medical diagnosis, and uses it to solve problems.

factorial A term referring to a number multiplied by all the positive integers smaller than it. For example, six factorial, indicated as "6!", would be $6 \times 5 \times 4 \times 3 \times 2 \times 1$, or 720.

forward chaining Working from the beginning of a problem to the end, that is, reasoning from the given facts to reach a conclusion.

frame A way of organizing knowledge about a given domain in an AI program so that it can be accessed. A frame has a branching structure. The information is more specific as the branches get progressively finer.

heuristic A "rule of thumb" used to help find solutions to problems. Heuristics are needed to help limit the search for a solution and to choose possible paths, among other things. Use of a heuristic will not necessarily lead to a solution.

knowledge base The factual information contained in an AI program.

LIPS Logic Inferences Per Second, the measuring unit of speed for the new logic-based computers.

LISP The most popular language for AI programs in the United States. LISP programs are organized as lists of data and procedures.

LOGO A computer language similar to LISP but with extended graphics capability.

minimax algorithm An algorithm often used in game programs that assumes the opponent will always select the best move. The possible moves for the computer and the opponent are given numerical values, calculated by static evaluation functions, based on how advantageous the moves are. By examining these numbers, the computer can choose the move that will result in the best position several moves later.

monotonic logic Standard logic that does not allow for the answer "I don't know."

natural language Language as it is commonly used by people in conversation or writing.

node A branch point in a search tree.

nonmonotonic logic Logic that allows qualifying statements to be made, so that a particular statement may be applicable under some circumstances and not others.

object In certain computer languages such as Smalltalk, a thing or a concept around which characteristics can be organized. In a game program, for example, "courage" could be an object associated with traits such as "fights to the death," "never runs away," and so forth.

parser The part of a language understanding program that takes apart a sentence and analyzes the grammar.

production rules IF . . . THEN statements used in certain AI programs to search for solutions. If the condition (the "if" part of the rule) is met by the data, the "then" part of the rule is applied. Production rules are the foundation of AI systems called "production systems." Production rules are especially useful in expert systems. For example, a production rule could read, "IF the patient has a fever of over 105°, THEN examine the other symptoms to check for meningitis."

PROLOG An increasingly popular language used for AI. It is organized around logic.

rule base A set of production rules in a production system such as an expert system.

script In AI programming, a collection of facts about a specific type of situation, such as going to a restaurant, that tells the program what to expect under the circumstances. Scripts are one way of providing a program with some commonsense knowledge.

search tree The branching set of possible alternatives in an AI program. Because the number of alternatives increases exponentially at each level, the search tree gets very large very fast (see **combinatorial explosion**), and ways of limiting the number of alternatives are keys to successful AI programs.

semantics The meaning of a string of words, including the correct connotations.

SHRDLU An AI system devised by Terry Winograd that manipulates blocks in a "blocks' world" environment. Because its world is so limited, SHRDLU is able to exhibit some commonsense reasoning.

Smalltalk An object-based computer language (see **object**) that can be used for AI programs.

static evaluation function A mathematical relation that calculates a numerical value for the relative merits of different moves in game programs.

ULSI chip A chip so packed with circuits (Ultra Large Scale Integration) that it can hold over one million K of memory.

variable A symbol used to indicate something that can have different values under different conditions. For example, the variable "color" could be used in noting a person's hair. The variable color could have many values— black, brown, blond, gray, and so forth—depending on who was being described.

VLSI chip A computer chip that is packed with an enormous number of circuits (Very Large Scale Integration). A VLSI chip can hold up to one million K of memory.

Sources for Information
and Quotations

I relied heavily on certain sources for information in particular sections of the book, and I wish to thank the authors for their clear and interesting explanations of their material.

Elaine Rich, Ch. 1: *Artificial Intelligence*, McGraw Hill, N.Y., 1983.

Roger Schank and Larry Hunter, Ch. 1: *Byte*, April, 1985, p. 155.

ELIZA dialog, Ch. 3: *Communications of the Association for Computing Machinery*, Volume 9, 1965, pp. 36–45.

Discussion of ELIZA and Racter, Ch. 3: "Computer Recreations," by A. K. Dewdney, *Scientific American*, January, 1985.

Racter/ELIZA dialog, Ch. 3: *Scientific American*, January, 1985, p. 16.

Problems in Ch. 4: Elaine Rich, *Artificial Intelligence*, and Nils J. Nilsson, *Principles of Artificial Intelligence*, Tioga Publishing Co., Palo Alto, CA, 1980.

Discussion of AI languages, Ch. 5: "Metamagical Themas," by Douglas R. Hofstadter, *Scientific American*, February, 1983; "Computer Languages of the Future," by Jonathan Amsterdam, *Popular Computing*, September, 1983.

Douglas Lenat, Ch. 6: *Scientific American*, September, 1984, p. 207.

Samuel's checkers program, Ch. 8: *The Handbook of Artificial Intelligence* (see Suggested Reading).

Rex, by Harl Vincent, Ch. 10: *Machines That Think*, Isaac Asimov, ed., Holt, Rinehart and Winston, N.Y., 1984, p. 50; originally published in *Astounding Stories* in 1934.

Parsers in computer games, Ch. 11: "Interactive Fiction," by Shay Addams, *Popular Computing*, March, 1985.

Roger Schank, Ch. 12: *Science*, vol. 223, 1984, p. 805.

Hubert Dreyfus, Ch. 12: "Computer Culture," *Annuals of the N.Y. Academy of Sciences*, Vol. 426; 1984, p. 145; second quote p. 158.

Edward Feigenbaum, Ch. 12: *Science*, vol. 223, 1984, p. 804.

Roger Schank, Allen Newell, and Geoffrey Hinton, Ch. 13: *Science*, vol. 225, 1984, p. 610.

Seymour Papert, Ch. 14: *Psychology Today*, December, 1983, p. 28, and "Computer Culture," p. 150.

A. Sloman, Ch. 14: *Artificial Intelligence, Human Effects*, M. Yazdani and A. Narayanan, eds., Ellis Horwood Ltd., West Sussex, England, 1984, p. 180.

John McCarthy, Ch. 14: *Psychology Today*, December, 1983, p. 49.

Joseph Weizenbaum, Ch. 14: *Computer Power and Human Reason*, Joseph Weizenbaum, p. 6–7.

Terry Winograd, Ch. 14: "The Ethics of Artificial Intelligence," by Joel Shurkin, *The Stanford Observer*, January, 1985.

Suggested Reading

General Books

Asimov, Isaac. *Robots: Machines in Man's Image*. Harmony Books (Crown), New York, 1985. A survey of robots, including their history and their future.

Dreyfus, Hubert. *What Computers Can't Do: A Critique of Artificial Reason*. Harper and Row, New York, 1979. A philosopher looks critically at the concept of artificial intelligence.

Dreyfus, Hubert and Stuart Dreyfus. *Mind Over Machine: The Power of Human Intuition and Expertise in the Era of the Computer*. The Free Press, New York, 1985. A philosopher and a computer scientist collaborate in a discussion of the role of computers.

Feigenbaum, Edward A. and Pamela McCorduck. *The Fifth Generation*. Addison-Wesley, Reading, MA, 1983. A discussion of the Japanese Fifth Generation project; also general information on AI and expert systems.

McCorduck, Pamela. *Machines Who Think*. W. H. Freeman, San Francisco, 1979. A history of AI, from the first ideas of philosophers about thinking machines up to 1979.

Racter. *The Policeman's Beard Is Half-Constructed*. Warner Books, Inc., N.Y., 1984. A collection of Racter's writings.

Ritchie, David. *The Binary Brain*. Little, Brown and Company, Boston, 1984. Discusses brains, computers, and AI.

Rose, Frank. *Into the Heart of the Mind.* Harper & Row, New York, 1984. An interesting essay about work in natural language understanding being carried out at the University of California at Berkeley.

Schank, Roger C., with Peter G. Childers. *The Cognitive Computer.* Addison-Wesley, Reading, MA, 1984. Human intelligence and machine intelligence are discussed by the director of the Yale University Artificial Intelligence Project.

Turkle, Sherry. *The Second Self: Computers and the Human Spirit.* Simon and Schuster, New York, 1984. Explores the attitudes of the public and specialists toward computers. Includes an interesting section on AI.

Weizenbaum, Joseph. *Computer Power and Human Reason.* W. H. Freeman, San Francisco, 1976. An artificial intelligence pioneer discusses the problems of relating to computers as machines with great power.

More Technical Books

Boden, Margaret. *Artificial Intelligence and Natural Man.* Basic Books, New York, 1977. An investigation of the nature of computers and the nature of humans.

Cohen, Paul R. and Edward A. Feigenbaum, editors. *The Handbook of Artificial Intelligence.* Three volumes. William Kaufmann, Inc., Los Altos, CA, 1982. Discusses the basic problems of AI such as searching, representing knowledge, and understanding natural language. While much of the information is technical, a great deal is understandable to the interested nonspecialist.

Krutch, John. *Experiments in Artificial Intelligence for Small Computers.* Howard W. Sams & Co., Inc., Indianapolis, IN, 1982. The programs are written in BASIC, but they illustrate the elementary techniques of writing AI programs.

Magazine Articles

Various authors. "Artificial Intelligence," *Byte*, April, 1985. Contains a number of articles on different aspects of AI, including "The Quest to Understand Thinking," by Roger Schank and Larry Hunter (p. 143) and "Reverse Engineering the Brain," by John K. Stevens (p. 286).

Various authors. "User Friendly," *Psychology Today*, December, 1983. Several articles about AI, including "The Little Thoughts of Thinking Machines," by John McCarthy (p. 46) and "The Well-Tempered Robot," by Howard Rheingold (p. 38).

Berliner, Hans. "Computer Backgammon," *Scientific American*, June, 1980. A discussion of game programs, with emphasis on Berliner's backgammon work.

Dewdney, A. K. "Computer Recreations, Artificial Insanity," *Scientific American*, January, 1985. A discussion of Racter and how the program works.

Hofstadter, Douglas R. "Metamagical Themas," February, March, and April, 1983, *Scientific American*. In these three columns, Hofstadter gives a thorough discussion of LISP and how it is used in AI programs.

Lerner, Eric J. "Robotics: The Birth of Vision," *Science Digest*, July, 1985. A look at visual systems for mobile robots under development at Carnegie-Mellon University.

Poggio, Tomaso. "Vision by Man and Machine," *Scientific American*, April, 1984. The problems of "seeing" machines are explained, with several examples of attempts to deal with them.

Raibert, Marc H. and Ivan E. Sutherland. "Machines That Walk," *Scientific American*, January, 1983. Discusses the problem of animal locomotion and one attempt to design a machine that walks.

Rose, Frank. "The Black Knight of AI," *Science 85*, March, 1985. Discusses Hubert Dreyfus' criticisms of AI.

Waldrop, M. Mitchell. "The Machinations of Thought," *Science 85*, March, 1985. A general overview of AI.

Microcomputer Software

ELIZA. Artificial Intelligence Research Group, 921 North La Jolla Avenue, Los Angeles, CA 90046. This version is not, however, identical to the one mentioned in this book.

Racter. Mindscape, 3444 Dundee Road, Northbrook, ILL 60062. This version is not, however, identical to the one mentioned in this book.

Acknowledgments

I want to thank Drs. Robert Franklin, Paul Martin, Hans Berliner, Bruce Clayton, and J. Mark Wright for the helpful information they gave me during this project. Thanks also to Barbara Baird and Greg and Jason Patent for their comments on the manuscript. Special appreciation goes to Drs. Kenneth Silvestro and Richard Lane, who read parts of the manuscript for accuracy and made many useful suggestions.

Index

Numbers in italics refer to illustrations.